Optimal Well-Being for Senior Adults I

Reproducible Activity Handouts Promoting Healthy Life Skills

Ester R.A. Leutenberg
Kathy A. Khalsa, CPC, OTR/L

Illustrated by
Amy L. Brodsky, LISW-S

Mandala Art by
Esther Piszczek, CZT

wholeperson
Health & Wellness Publishers

101 West 2nd Street, Suite 203
Duluth, MN 55802

800-247-6789

books@WholePerson.com
WholePerson.com

Optimal Well-Being for Senior Adults I
Reproducible Activity Handouts Promoting Healthy Life Skills

Copyright ©2016 by Ester R.A. Leutenberg and Kathy A. Khalsa. All rights reserved. The activities, assessment tools, and handouts in this book are reproducible by the purchaser for educational or therapeutic purposes. No other part of this book may be reproduced or transmitted in any form by any means, electronic or mechanical without permission in writing from the publisher.

All efforts have been made to ensure accuracy of the information contained in this book as of the date published. The author(s) and the publisher expressly disclaim responsibility for any adverse effects arising from the use or application of the information contained herein.

Printed in the United States of America
10 9 8 7 6 5 4 3 2 1

Editorial Director: Carlene Sippola
Art Director: Mathew Pawlak
Mandala Design: Esther Piszczek, CZT
Illustrator: Amy L. Brodsky, LISW-S

Library of Congress Control Number: 2016932442
ISBN:978-157025-343-0

Optimal Well-Being for Senior Adults I
Introduction

Optimal Well-Being for Senior Adults I is the first in a series of workbooks consisting of reproducible activity handouts that will meet the needs of both facilitators and their clients. The activities in the workbook are clear, easy-to-follow handouts written for mental health professionals to provide guidance and content to their senior clients.

It is written with the intent to be adapted, if needed, and then reproduced for an individual or a group. The handouts can be individualized to meet the specific needs of the participants. Creativity is encouraged by both the leader and participants in an ongoing process to generate satisfying and meaningful sessions.

The use of artwork, graphics, and different fonts offers interest and variety to enhance focus and attention to the topic at hand.

To aid the facilitator, each handout has a Leader's Guide written for the facilitator. It includes the following:
- **Purpose** (identify the skill the participant will be learning)
- **Possible Names of Sessions** (offers the name of the session or choices from three other names)
- **Background Information** (can be used as a brief introduction for the session)
- **Activity** (provides a step-by-step outline for how to lead a session)
- **Variations** (describes at least one variation different from the outlined activity)

Each of the ten chapters has five handouts with three levels of understanding.
This format encourages the facilitator to choose which level is most appropriate for the specific individuals to be served and avoid frustration of both the facilitator and group members.

Within each chapter the five handouts consist of …
- One handout: a Basic Level of understanding, which provides more concrete and less abstract language and concepts.
- Three handouts: an Intermediate Level of understanding for individuals who can easily sustain concentration and focus.
- One handout: a High Level of understanding to be used with individuals with a high ability for listening, sharing and developing insight.

The level of understanding icons will be on the cover page of each chapter and on the back of the activity handouts entitled The Leader's Guide.

The activity handouts for the participants are all …
- Activity-based allowing for client involvement
- Designed for specific, well-defined purposes
- Organized logically
- Reproducible
- User-friendly
- Visually appealing

The certificate on page 131 may be photocopied, filled in, and awarded to participants when they have completed their handouts.

Although this workbook is intended for senior adults, often referring to the 50+ age group, others may benefit from it as well.

10 Valuable Tips for Facilitating Senior Adult Groups

Some helpful tips to consider when leading groups with seniors to ensure effective outcomes and preemptively manage your possible frustration level:

1. At the beginning of the group session, establish if everyone can hear properly by asking, "Can everyone hear me?" If people answer "no," consider rearranging the seating to allow those who cannot hear to sit in another place, or you as the group leader, can change seats. If the people who sit across from you have seats with their backs to the wall, they might find that this improves their ability to hear.

2. Have an assortment of different pens and pencils to accommodate fine-motor coordination. Black pens will be easiest to read, especially with people who have visual impairments.

3. If the group room does not have tables, have magazines or clipboards handy to provide sturdy writing surfaces.

4. For organizational purposes, photocopy and then three-hole punch the handouts. Distribute three-hole folders or notebooks, or have pocket folders available for each participant.

5. To save time and allow yourself to be prepared, organize handouts by levels in three notebooks:
   - One notebook for basic level handouts (10 handouts)
   - One notebook for intermediate level handouts (30 handouts)
   - One notebook for high level handouts (10 handouts)

   This will allow you to quickly and easily find the appropriate handouts. You may also divide notebooks between topics to offer the most appropriate handout to a specific group or individual.

6. Be aware of bathroom needs and accommodate the times of your groups accordingly.

7. If the ambient noise around the group interferes, make a sign saying "SHHHH … Group in Progress" to cue staff to lower their voices. Place the sign where the people passing by can easily see it.

8. If you determine during the group session that the handout and activity you chose was too difficult, or too easy, quickly adapt it rather than continuing. Find an easier or more challenging way to present the content of the handout, or have a plan B already photocopied and ready to go to avoid everyone (including you as the facilitator) from being frustrated.

9. Feel free to elaborate on any topic provided. For example, when you present on the topic of humor, relate to the group what you have recently read or experienced. For instance: "I recently read an article that pointed out that laughter can be the best medicine … it's good for your heart, immune system, brain health, and increases pain tolerance."

10. At the end of the session, ask group members what they learned or relearned from the session. In addition to gaining valuable feedback, it is useful for documentation purposes.

INTRODUCTION

Table of Contents – Sorted by Topics

Topic I – Anxiety and Stress 9
Stress Symptoms 11
Anxiety 13
Stress Management – Past & Present 15
Stress Relief - A to Z 17
Anxiety: Mind-Racing 19

Topic II – Coping 21
My Inner Circle 23
Don't Put All Your Eggs in One Basket . . . 25
Making Transitions 27
Purposeful Activity 29
Senior Adults as Survivors and Copers . . . 31

Topic III – Emotion Expression 33
Talk About Feelings 35
Effects of Emotional Abuse 37
If I Could Write a Book
  About My Life 39
My Rights as a Senior Adult 41
Reveal How You Feel 43

Topic IV – Grief and Loss 45
Grief Grabs You 47
Grief Feels Like 49
Inside Outside 51
Steps of Grief 53
Healing from Loss 55

Topic V – Life Balance 57
Find the Balance for Next Week 59
Keeping on Schedule 61
Turn the Da _ _ TV Off! 63
What is One More Thing? 65
Weekly Schedule 67

Topic VI – Reminiscence 69
Sing, Sing a Song 71
I'll Never Forget the Day 73
Remember These Sayings? 75
Slogans 77
You and Historic Dates 79

Topic VII – Self-Awareness 81
Celebrate You! 83
Give Yourself a Pat on the Back 85
How I Grew to Be Who I Am 87
Seeing My Strengths 89
How Does Your Garden Grow? 91

Topic VIII – Social Skills 93
Celebrating the Seasons 95
A Dozen Effective
  Communication Tips 97
Acts of Loving Kindness 99
The Social Skills Interview 101
What I Like to Do 103

Topic IX – Staying Young at Heart   105
Finding Humor Today! 107
Empowering Myself to Be Active 109
Energy Conservation 111
I Want My Independence 113
What Can I Do 115

Topic X – Thinking Skills 117
The "AND" Game 119
The "AND" Game – Challenge Edition . . 121
Current Events 123
Which / Witch is It? 125
Mental Toughness – The Thinker Quiz . . 127

Bonus 129
Certificate 131
Mandala 133

Table of Contents
Activity Handouts Sorted in Alphabetical Order

Activity Handout	Topic	Page
A Dozen Effective Communication Tips	Social Skills	97
Acts of Loving Kindness	Social Skills	99
Anxiety	Anxiety and Stress	13
Anxiety: Mind-Racing	Anxiety and Stress	19
Celebrate You!	Self-Awareness	83
Celebrating the Seasons	Social Skills	95
Certificate	Bonus	131
Current Events	Thinking Skills	123
Don't Put All Your Eggs in One Basket	Coping	25
Effects of Emotional Abuse	Emotion Expression	37
Empowering Myself to Be Active	Staying Young at Heart	109
Energy Conservation	Staying Young at Heart	111
Find the Balance for Next Week	Life Balance	59
Finding Humor Today!	Staying Young at Heart	107
Give Yourself a Pat on the Back	Self-Awareness	85
Grief Feels Like	Grief and Loss	49
Grief Grabs You	Grief and Loss	47
Healing from Loss	Grief and Loss	55
How Does Your Garden Grow?	Self-Awareness	91
How I Grew to Be Who I Am	Self-Awareness	87
I Want My Independence	Staying Young at Heart	113
I'll Never Forget the Day	Reminiscence	73
If I Could Write a Book About My Life	Emotion Expression	39
Inside Outside	Grief and Loss	51
Keeping on Schedule	Life Balance	61
Making Transitions	Coping	27
Mandala	Bonus	133
Mental Toughness – The Thinker Quiz	Thinking Skills	127
My Inner Circle	Coping	23
My Rights as a Senior Adult	Emotion Expression	41
Purposeful Activity	Coping	29
Remember These Sayings?	Reminiscence	75
Reveal How You Feel	Emotion Expression	43
Seeing My Strengths	Self-Awareness	89
Senior Adults as Survivors and Copers	Coping	31
Sing, Sing a Song	Reminiscence	71
Slogans	Reminiscence	77
Steps of Grief	Grief and Loss	53
Stress Management – Past & Present	Anxiety and Stress	15
Stress Relief A to Z	Anxiety and Stress	17
Stress Symptoms	Anxiety and Stress	11
Talk About Feelings	Emotion Expression	35
The "AND" Game	Thinking Skills	119
The "AND" Game – Challenge Edition	Thinking Skills	121
The Social Skills Interview	Social Skills	101
Turn the Da _ _ TV Off!	Life Balance	63
Weekly Schedule	Life Balance	67
What Can I Do	Staying Young at Heart	115
What I Like to Do	Social Skills	103
What is One More Thing?	Life Balance	65
Which / Witch is It?	Thinking Skills	125
You and Historic Dates	Reminiscence	79

INTRODUCTION

> *We dedicate this workbook to those senior adults*
> *who have inspired us in the past, who inspire us today,*
> *and to those, we are confident,*
> *will continue to inspire us in the future.*
>
> *Esther Leutenberg   Kathy Khalsa*

Our thanks to the following professionals who make us look good!

Art Director – Mathew Pawlak
Editorial Director – Carlene Sippola
Illustrator – Amy L. Brodsky, LISW-S
Mandala Art – Esther Piszczek, CZT
Editor and Lifelong Teacher – Eileen Regen, MEd, CJE
Proofreader – Jay Leutenberg, CASA
Reviewer – Carol Butler, MS Ed, RN, C
Contributor – Kris Lowden, MA
Researcher – Sophia Korb, PhD

Thanks to
The Guidance Group

and to the
Meaningful Life Skills contributors

Sandra Christensen, BA
Kim Corbett, OTR/L
Marta Felber, M Ed
Kelly Fischer, OTR/L
Martin B. Golub, CTRS
Mary Lou Hamilton, MS, RN
Kimberly D. Heath, MA
K. Oscar Larson, OTR, MA, BCG
Judith A. Lutz, BA
Mark S. Macko, M Ed
Esterlee A. Molyneux, M, SSW
Libby D. Schardt, OTR/L
Sylvia T. Schwartzman, RN, MS
Wanda M. Verne, BSPM

Topic I
ANXIETY AND STRESS
Table of Contents and Corresponding Goals for Each Section

Don't believe everything you think. Thoughts are just that – thoughts.
~ Allan Lokos

Stress Symptoms 11
To identify personal stress symptoms and positive ways to cope.

Anxiety 13
To explore non-pharmacological methods of managing anxiety.

STRESS MANAGEMENT – PAST AND PRESENT 15
To explore past messages about stress management that may contribute to current stress management.

Stress Relief A to Z 17
To explore relaxation and stress reduction techniques.

Anxiety Mind-Racing 19
To examine mind-racing using an insight-oriented approach.

LEVEL OF UNDERSTANDING — Basic Level, Intermediate Level, High Level

Topic I — ANXIETY AND STRESS

Stress Symptoms

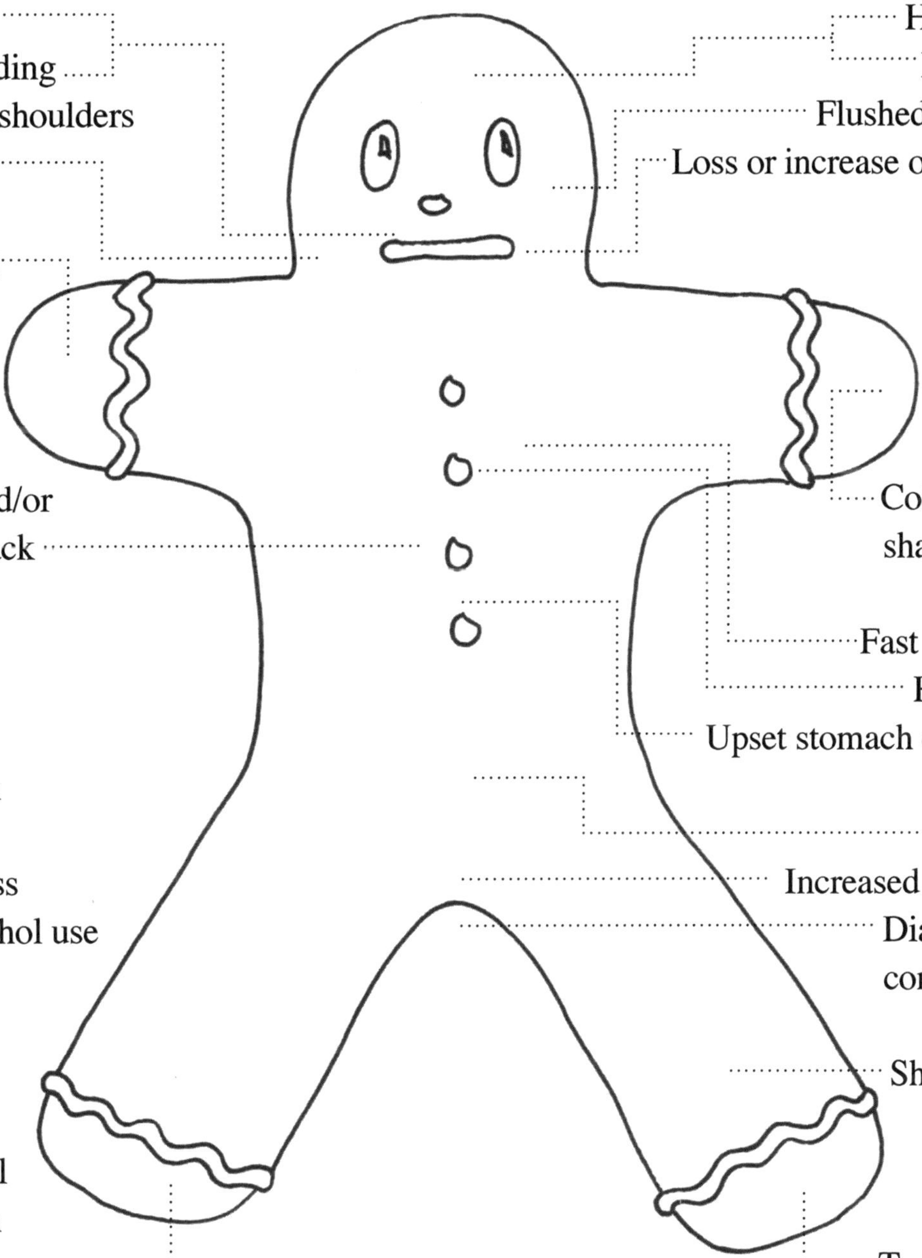

__ Dry mouth
__ Teeth Grinding
__ Tension in shoulders and neck

__ Nail Biting

__ Tension and/or aches in back

__ Crying
__ Depression
__ Smoking
__ Restlessness
__ Drugs/alcohol use

__ Withdrawal
__ Aggression
__ Boredom
__ Decreased concentration
__ Sleep increase or decrease
__ Impulsivity

Headaches __
Dizziness __
Flushed, hot face __
Loss or increase of appetite __

Cold or shaky hands __

Fast heartbeat __
Heartburn __
Upset stomach or nausea __

Cramps __
Increased urination __
Diarrhea or constipation __

Shaky Legs __

Tapping feet __

OPTIMAL WELL-BEING FOR SENIOR ADULTS I

Stress Symptoms
Leader's Guide

PURPOSE
To identify personal stress symptoms and positive ways to cope.

POSSIBLE NAMES OF SESSIONS
- Stress … In My Body?
- I FEEL My Stress
- Stress Can Hurt!

BACKGROUND INFORMATION
Stress can manifest itself in a variety of different symptoms. The ways that individuals deal with stress is as unique as the way it presents itself to them. This activity provides the opportunity to identify personal stress symptoms and positive ways to handle them.

ACTIVITY
1. Ask group members to define 'stress,' and what it means to be 'stressed-out.'
2. Distribute handouts.
3. Ask group members to check the symptoms that occur when they feel stressed.
4. Discuss the benefits of identifying stress symptoms and how this leads to prevention.
5. Discuss the mind-body connection and the fact that when someone has a sore back, the back pain increases when that person feels stressed.
6. Brainstorm a list of ways to manage stress. The following are some examples.
   a. Relaxation techniques (abdominal breathing, progressive muscles relaxation, imagery, yoga, etc.)
   b. Aerobic exercise
   c. Proper food plan and nutrition
   d. Cognitive restructuring (replacing negative or self-defeating thoughts with a positive, gentle mind-set)
   e. Increase emotional expression. (verbal and written)
   f. Emotional support (friends, family, counselors)
   g. Self-nurturance (take time for yourself with pleasurable activities)
   h. Elimination of drugs and/or alcohol
   i. Development of preventative habits (priority setting, time management)
   j. Learning to tolerate and forgive
   k. Decrease perfectionistic behavior
7. Process the benefits of the group.

VARIATIONS
1) Before the activity, draw a large human figure on a dry erase board. Ask group members where they feel stress in their bodies. Mark on corresponding parts of the figure.
2) Make a video of a helpful technique for members to use in the future.
3) Serve gingerbread men cookies for a treat after session.

NOTES
_____
_____
_____

Topic I — ANXIETY AND STRESS

Anxiety

Anxiety
can be described as nervousness, tension, dread, fearfulness, agitation, high sensitivity.

Anxiety
may be an exaggerated response stemming from past events that have little to do with the here and now.

Anxiety
is a response to fears and worries, loss of control, a desire for everything to be perfect, an exaggerated need for approval. It may arise after one has ignored signs of stress.

When the quality, intensity and duration of anxiety is too much, it can result in anxiety symptoms. Some anxiety symptoms to notice:
- Fast, shallow breathing
- Muscular tension
- Mind-racing
- Loss of concentration
- Poor sleep

What are some of your anxiety symptoms?

- _____
- _____
- _____
- _____

Although medications can be taken, non-pharmacological methods are also very useful, AND they have no side effects! Think of the mind-body connection and try these relaxation therapy techniques.

Relaxation Therapy Techniques	Before 1 = low anxiety 10 = high anxiety	My Response After 1 = low anxiety 10 = high anxiety
Progressive Muscle Relaxation		
Guided Imagery		
Mindful Breathing		

Anxiety
Leader's Guide

PURPOSE
To explore non-pharmacological methods of managing anxiety.

POSSIBLE NAMES OF SESSIONS
- ANXIETY …My Choices
- The Mind-Body Connection
- Breathe Away

BACKGROUND INFORMATION
Anxiety often accompanies medical and psychiatric illnesses. It can be a serious medical condition that affects all areas of functioning. Although pharmacological means can be effective, some can have adverse side effects and be addictive.

ACTIVITY
1. Review information provided in the Background Information.
2. Distribute handouts and pens.
3. Discuss individual symptoms and list on dry erase board.
4. Explore the three relaxation possibilities, each in a ten-minute session. After each trial, allow individuals to comment briefly and to write a personal response. Explain that a rating response activity before and after each session will be a helpful way to measure their anxiety levels.
5. Adjust each group experience to the physical limitations of the members and adapt accordingly. Consider hearing limitations, ROM (Range of Motion) limitations, etc.
6. Support group members in finding at least one relaxation exercise that will be helpful.
7. Discuss ways that each group member can continue the most beneficial methods in the future.

VARIATIONS
1) Bring to the group a staff member or client who has mastered any of the three relaxation techniques explored, to present the benefits, and to demonstrate and lead an exercise.
2) Provide resources to ensure helpful techniques are accessible for members to use in the future.

NOTES
_____
_____
_____
_____
_____
_____
_____
_____
_____
_____
_____

Topic I — ANXIETY AND STRESS

STRESS MANAGEMENT — PAST AND PRESENT

The lessons we learned in our past inform us on how we manage stress now. Below, respond to the following questions about your past and present.

Past	Present
1. Think back to your childhood. How did the adults in your life manage their stress?	1. What was one way in the last month that you managed stress?
2. As a child or teenager, how did you manage your stress?	2. When you are at home, what is one stress management activity that is immediately accessible?
3. What is a memory from your childhood or teen years when you managed stress in an unhealthy way?	3. Who is one person in your life, who can support you in managing stress well?
4. What is a memory from your childhood or teen years when you managed stress in a healthy way?	4. What is one goal or boundary that you can set to assist you in stress management?
5. How does your past affect your stress management today?	5. Who are role models for you, who manage or managed their stress well in their older years?

How did the lessons you learned in your past inform how you manage stress now?

OPTIMAL WELL-BEING FOR SENIOR ADULTS I

STRESS MANAGEMENT – PAST AND PRESENT
Leader's Guide

PURPOSE
To explore past messages about stress management that may contribute to current stress management.

POSSIBLE NAMES OF SESSIONS
- *What I Learned as a Kid About Stress*
- *Stress: Then and Now*
- *Stress: I'm NOT My Past!*

BACKGROUND INFORMATION
Stress management styles of adults are observed by children. It is important to look back at these lessons learned to see if stress management styles of today may have been influenced by the past. With awareness, stress management styles can be understood with a degree of compassion and then modified.

ACTIVITY
1. Help group members see that children learn from observing adults by simply observing their behaviors. Ask group members to think back to their childhoods. "How did adults manage their money?" Draw a parallel: They also learned messages about stress management.
2. Distribute handouts and pens. Ask group members to complete the handout.
3. Discuss responses and explain that this exercise is not intended for group members to blame their pasts for the lessons learned. Instead it is to be aware of how their stress management responses may feel automatic and natural, and for them to realize that they do not need to stay that way. Healthy choices can be made today.

VARIATIONS
1) Discuss different ways children may have observed adults manage stress: alcohol, violence, blaming, shutting down, silent treatment, rage, walking out, etc. Emphasize how children are perceptive to their environments and pick up on both subtle and obvious clues.
2) Discuss this quote by Abraham Maslow: "In any given moment, we have two options: to step forward into growth or to step back into safety."

NOTES
_____
_____
_____
_____
_____
_____
_____
_____
_____
_____
_____

Stress Relief A to Z

Topic I — ANXIETY AND STRESS

A to Z Examples	Your Own Stress Relief A to Z Suggestions
Avoid negative people.	A
Be yourself.	B
Change your thought.	C
Don't think you know all the answers.	D
Exercise often.	E
Feed the birds.	F
Give someone a hug.	G
Hum a joyful song.	H
Invite a friend to dinner.	I
Join others when invited.	J
Keep a journal.	K
Look up at the stars.	L
Make duplicate car or house keys.	M
NO! Just say it with no excuses.	N
Open a door for someone.	O
Pet a friendly dog or cat.	P
Quit trying to fix other people.	Q
Repair things that don't work properly.	R
Stand up and stretch.	S
Take a shower.	T
Use time wisely.	U
Visualize yourself relaxing.	V
Walk in the rain.	W
X-plore a new idea.	X
Yak with a friend.	Y
Zoom into a healthy restaurant.	Z

OPTIMAL WELL-BEING FOR SENIOR ADULTS I

Stress Relief A to Z
Leader's Guide

PURPOSE
To explore relaxation and stress reduction techniques.

POSSIBLE NAMES OF SESSIONS
- *Reduce Your Stress – Alphabetically De-Stressing*
- *Create 26 New Stress Strategies*
- *The A-B-C's of Stress Management*

BACKGROUND INFORMATION
When we are feeling overly stressed we tend to forget to do the things that we need to do to take care of ourselves – things that we enjoy and find relaxing. Self-care is often the first thing to go. Taking care of ourselves breaks the cycle of our stress. Interrupting the cycle of our stress is an important stress-management strategy.

ACTIVITY
1. Introduce the topic of stress (or anxiety) management using the background information. Discuss the importance and benefits of self-management strategies to overall health, relationships, and quality of life.
2. Distribute handouts and pens.
3. Ask a volunteer to read from the left side of the page (or, to make it more interesting, have volunteers pantomime role-play for each as it is read).
4. Instruct the group to develop their own Stress Relief A to Z on the right side of the page. Encourage creativity or nonsense words for the more difficult letters (see the letter Y).
5. Instruct group members to read their responses and discuss how each one helps with stress relief.

VARIATIONS
1) Before the activity, discuss the concept that if we always do what we have done in the past, we are likely to get the same results. Go around the room and ask each person, "When you are stressed out, what do you do consistently that does not bring good results?" Then ask, "What can you do the next time this happens?"
2) Divide the group into teams of 3-4 group members. Distribute handouts and pens to each team. Ask each team to complete the right side of the page. Give one point for each technique that is not listed by other groups. The winning team gets a round of applause.
3) Assign different letters to group members, encouraging them to brainstorm as many stress relievers as they can in 60 seconds.

NOTES
_____
_____
_____
_____
_____
_____
_____
_____

Topic I — ANXIETY AND STRESS

Anxiety Mind-Racing

Anxiety can often feel like your mind is running away …
going faster and faster and faster …
but not getting anywhere!

Here are some thought-provoking questions to help you look at your worries more clearly:

What are you most worried about? _____

_____

What is the likelihood that this will happen?   1_____2_____3_____4_____5
                                                           NOT VERY LIKELY   VERY LIKELY

Do you have any control of the outcome?   ☐ YES   ☐ NO
- If your response is NO, focus on acceptance and the wisdom that is required.
- If your response is NO, recognize that your control in the matter may be limited by a variety of factors. Your insights will help you manage your anxiety with the following strategies:
- If your response is YES, do your part and then recognize when it is no longer in your control.

JOURNAL … TALK … USE A RELAXATION TECHNIQUE …
FIND A DISTRACTION … MEDITATE …
ENGAGE IN SLOW BREATHING … EXERCISE … STRETCH

Anxiety Mind-Racing
Leader's Guide

PURPOSE
To examine mind-racing using an insight-oriented approach.

POSSIBLE NAMES OF SESSIONS
- *Does Worrying Make It Better?*
- *What If …*
- *Mind-Racing Gets Me Nowhere*

BACKGROUND INFORMATION
Mind-racing is characterized by fast-paced thoughts. One thought replaces another and then the mind becomes overactive. At times, worries repeat themselves.

ACTIVITY
1. Ask group members to relate their worries, and ask for a volunteer to write them on a board.
2. Acknowledge that each worry is significant.
3. Distribute handouts and pens.
4. Give group members ample time to discuss their responses.
5. As a group, choose a strategy from the bottom of the page to explore. Facilitate that strategy, and then process.
6. Encourage using a strategy before bedtime when mind-racing may escalate, except exercising, which is better done earlier in the day.

VARIATIONS
1) Find a video of a gerbil on an exercise wheel on an Internet site. Introduce mind-racing and then the video at the beginning of the group for some comic relief as the group members relate to themselves and mind-racing.
2) Explore the "What ifs …" by discussing how to handle the worst-case scenarios.

NOTES

Topic II

COPING

Table of Contents and Corresponding Goals for Each Section

> *I guess in the end, it doesn't matter what we wanted.*
> *What matters is what we chose to do with the things we had.*
> ~ Mira Grant

My Inner Circle 23
To promote identification of supports and acknowledgement of their benefits.

Don't Put All Your Eggs in One Basket 25
To establish a coping skill incorporating leisure interests, spiritual supports, anger outlets, and social supports.

Making Transitions 27
To recognize the many different thoughts and feelings that accompany change.

To identify resources to help senior adults respond to change in a positive way.

Purposeful Activity 29
To explore a variety of distraction techniques and coping strategies that (might) work.

Senior Adults as Survivors and Copers 31
To facilitate coping skills in senior adults.

LEVEL OF UNDERSTANDING

 Basic Level    Intermediate Level    High Level

Topic II — COPING

My Inner Circle

**Who is in YOUR Circle?
Think of those closest to you.
Who can you count on if you need help?**

Place the name of one person in your life who matches the descriptions below in each of the shapes you choose, along with the phone number.

1. A family member
2. A neighbor
3. A spiritual support or someone with whom you really connect
4. A healthcare professional
5. A handy or helpful person, who knows how to get things done
6. YOUR CHOICE!

My Inner Circle
Leader's Guide

PURPOSE
To promote identification of supports and acknowledgement of their benefits.

POSSIBLE NAMES OF SESSIONS
- *Who's There For Me?*
- *Supports Come in All Shapes and Sizes*
- *Support Is Out There!*

BACKGROUND INFORMATION
It is important to take the time to see the possible different sources of supports in our lives. It may also be valuable (if not challenging) to assess the areas in which we lack supports and possible reasons for this. We all need the support of others; life is about giving and receiving in relationships. Having a visual reminder may serve as a lasting image of not being alone in our world.

ACTIVITY
1. Discuss the importance of having supports in our lives.
2. Discuss the nature of giving and receiving in relationships.
3. Distribute handouts and pens.
4. Give group members ten to fifteen minutes to complete the handout.
5. Encourage group members to investigate telephone numbers, if needed.
6. Ask group members to share their circles, and if there is time, tell why they chose their people.
7. Problem solve ways of developing new supports if some shapes are empty.

VARIATIONS
1) Look at the supports that were placed in certain shapes and discuss.
2) Discuss the YOUR CHOICE people. Were there commonalities among the chosen? Differences?

NOTES

Topic II — COPING

Don't Put All Your Eggs in One Basket

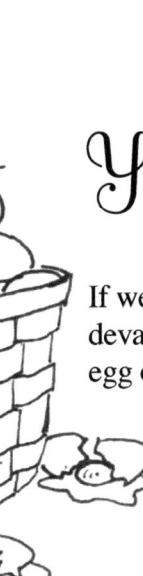

Life often presents unexpected challenges.
If we put all of our eggs in one basket, we may be disappointed, or even devastated, if an egg breaks, gets lost or misplaced. You never know when an egg or two may not be available.

Identify one egg from each category in each basket. All three baskets should have 4 eggs.
1. Leisure Interests
2. Spiritual Supports
3. Anger Outlets
4. Social Supports

Leisure Interests
_____

Spiritual Supports
_____

Anger Outlets
_____

Social Supports
_____

Leisure Interests
_____

Spiritual Supports
_____

Anger Outlets
_____

Social Supports
_____

Leisure Interests
_____

Spiritual Supports
_____

Anger Outlets
_____

Social Supports
_____

Don't Put All Your Eggs in One Basket
Leader's Guide

PURPOSE
To establish a coping skill incorporating leisure interests, spiritual supports, anger outlets, and social supports.

POSSIBLE NAMES OF SESSIONS
- *An Egg-sellent Way to Cope*
- *Scramble Those Eggs*
- *Egg-samples of a Coping Skill*

BACKGROUND INFORMATION
As we age, we might lose leisure interests, spiritual supports, anger outlets, and social supports. People move or pass away. Physical limitations prevent leisure and anger outlets. It is possible to take action to ensure that these important survival skills are still intact.

ACTIVITY
1. Bring three baskets, each with hard boiled eggs in them. On each egg write one of the following categories: leisure interests, spiritual supports, anger outlets, and social supports.
2. Explain the concept that if we put all of our eggs in one basket, and the basket gets lost, misplaced or destroyed, we would need another basket filled with the exact same things. Explain that as we age it is possible to lose the ability to engage in leisure interests, lose spiritual and social supports, and be unable to release our anger.
3. Offer an example of someone who loses the ability to play golf (due to a physical limitation). It is possible that this person lost a leisure interest, an anger outlet, and a social and a spiritual support. Discuss using relevant examples.
4. Distribute handouts and pens.
5. Divide group into pairs and instruct group members to complete handout. Give pairs an opportunity to share. If group members have eggs with nothing written on them, tell them that it's okay and there will be time for problem solving.
6. Tally results by asking, "Who had an egg with nothing written on it? What category was it in?" Proceed until you can group people together with the same needs.
7. Organize the large group into subgroups of people who need the same category.
8. Allow smaller subgroups to brainstorm ideas and support each other to fill in the blanks.
9. Reconvene and share results.

VARIATIONS
1) Discuss what other categories are recommended for healthy living.
2) Serve deviled eggs as a treat at the end of the group if diets or food plans allow.

NOTES
_____
_____
_____
_____
_____
_____
_____

Topic II — COPING

Making Transitions

Change is an inevitable part of life.
Some changes are welcome, resulting in feelings of excitement and joy.
Others are unwelcome and may result in anger, frustration, and/or despair.
Remember, change, even if it is a positive change, is still stressful.
Dealing with thoughts and feelings result in better decisions.
The goal is to make transitions smooth and successful!

What change or potential change is occurring in your life?
_____
_____

What are your thoughts about this change? _____
_____
_____

How do you feel about making this change? List as many feeling words as you can think of to describe your reaction to the change. _____
_____
_____
_____

Check (✔) the resources that can help you to respond more positively to changes in your life and explain how they can be supportive and/or beneficial.

☐ Family (Who?) _____

☐ Friends (Who?) _____

☐ Support group or counselor (Who?) _____

☐ Hobby (What?) _____

☐ Job or volunteer job (Describe) _____

☐ Faith Community (Describe) _____

☐ Myself (Check which of these following traits help you cope with change)

　　☐ Persistence　　☐ Positive Attitude　　☐ Sense of Humor

☐ Other resources _____

OPTIMAL WELL-BEING FOR SENIOR ADULTS I

Making Transitions
Leader's Guide

PURPOSE
To recognize the many different thoughts and feelings that accompany change.

To identify resources to help older adults address transitions in a positive way.

POSSIBLE NAMES OF SESSIONS
- *The Challenge of Change*
- *I've Never Done It This Way Before*
- *Transitions Can Be Tough*

BACKGROUND INFORMATION
Change is often a stressful part of life. Even desired changes can produce stress. By having a support system in place and developing personal coping strategies, aging adults will be better prepared to respond positively to this dynamic, and possibly challenging, time of life.

ACTIVITY
1. Review background information.
2. Discuss the possible changes people in this age group might be experiencing: children or grandchildren moving away; change in job status, financial situation, body or physical well-being; or loss of relationships. It may involve transition into retirement, moving from one's home or moving to an older adult community.
3. Distribute handouts and pens.
4. Ask group members to complete the top box.
5. Encourage group members to talk about the changes they are experiencing, as well as the feelings that accompany those changes.
6. Transition into a discussion of the lower box and encourage group members to complete. Invite the group to help each other identify resources that could assist them in responding to the changes in their lives with a positive attitude.

VARIATIONS
1) Encourage participants to identify at least one change that has occurred in their lifetimes, which at the beginning seemed to be viewed as a negative, but turned out to have some positive results.
2) Ask group members to talk about how their reactions to change have changed over time. What lessons have they learned over the years about how to cope with change?

NOTES
_____
_____
_____
_____
_____
_____
_____
_____
_____
_____

Purposeful Activity

Here are some distraction techniques and coping strategies that might work.

Feeling Angry and/or Frustrated?	Feeling Sad and/or Depressed?
Squeeze ice.	Do something slow and soothing.
Dance.	Take a shower.
Clean.	Baby yourself somehow.
Bang pots and pans.	Give yourself a treat or present.
Do something physical.	Play with a pet.
Talk about your feelings.	Make a list of what makes you happy.
Yell or sing at the top of your lungs.	Listen to soothing or uplifting music.
Play a sport.	Call or visit a friend.
Other	Other
Other	Other
Other	Other

Do Something Mindful!	Want Focus?
Count down slowly from 10 to 0.	Do a task that requires concentration.
Breathe slowly, in through the nose, and out through the mouth.	Find an interesting object. Sketch it with details.
Focus on objects around you, noticing how they look, sound, smell, taste and feel.	Pick a subject you are interested in and research it on the internet.
Do yoga.	Play a challenging game.
Meditate.	Read a short article. Write a summary in three sentences or less.
Other	Other
Other	Other
Other	Other

OPTIMAL WELL-BEING FOR SENIOR ADULTS I

Purposeful Activity
Leader's Guide

PURPOSE
To explore a variety of distraction techniques and coping strategies that (might) work.

POSSIBLE NAMES OF SESSIONS
- *Energy, Action, Purpose*
- *Being Purpose-full*
- *Actions Speak Louder Than Words*

BACKGROUND INFORMATION
Coping skills vary from person to person. They also change in their effectiveness across a lifespan. What worked well in our twenties may not work in our fifties or eighties. Learning distraction techniques and coping strategies is a trial and error process.

ACTIVITY
1. Place an ordinary collection of office supplies in the middle of the table (tape dispenser, stapler, pens, pencils, etc.)
2. Tell group members to draw a picture of the office supplies the best they can in two minutes.
3. Then, ask group members what happened to their worries, depression, or anger in the past two minutes. It is likely they will admit that distractions can be effective as a coping strategy.
4. Distribute handouts and pens, encouraging idea exploration and experimentation in the group.

VARIATIONS
1) Divide group into four subgroups. Each subgroup will discuss one of the four categories and find two of their favorite ideas to present. They will also add to the list provided with three additional ideas, and present them as well.
2) Prepare to do one idea from each of the four categories, as a group. Ask each group member to make a statement using the *talk about your feelings* prompt.
   "I feel frustrated when _____."
   or
   "I feel angry when _____."

NOTES
_____
_____
_____
_____
_____
_____
_____
_____
_____
_____
_____

Topic II — COPING

Senior Adults as Survivors and Copers

Some people might consider senior adults to be vulnerable and weak. But in fact, the opposite is true.	Senior adults have learned to survive. That's how they made it into their senior years!
Senior adults are survivors! They have coped through life's difficulties and challenging times!	Senior adults are copers! They can cope with what life throws their way.

SENIOR ADULTS

Do you feel as if you have survived through tough times? ☐ YES ☐ NO

If you answered yes, what were some of the tough times? _____
_____

What life lessons did you learn? _____
_____

What qualities or characteristics do you find in people who have overcome difficult times?
_____
_____

Which saying more aptly fits the way you see life?
 ☐ *When the going gets tough, the tough get going.* ☐ *Life is what you make of it.*

Who is a well-known celebrity, historical figure, or character in a book that you consider to be a survivor or coper? Explain. _____
_____

Which is more important to you, mental toughness or physical toughness? _____
Explain. _____
_____

If you could give one piece of advice to a twenty-year-old about how best to overcome life's difficult times, what would it be? _____
_____

OPTIMAL WELL-BEING FOR SENIOR ADULTS I

Senior Adults as Survivors and Copers
Leader's Guide

PURPOSE
To facilitate coping skills in senior adults.

POSSIBLE NAMES OF SESSIONS
- *Survival of the Fit?*
- *How DO the Tough Get Going?*
- *I Have Overcome*

BACKGROUND INFORMATION
The stereotype of senior adults being vulnerable and weak is perpetuated in the media and literature. As healthcare practitioners and educators, we can challenge this belief by acknowledging the strengths of surviving and coping with life's adversities. Senior adults may have experienced financial hard times, lack of personal choices, war, illness, and death of loved ones. Recognizing and praising a survivor's attitude may be a boost to foster resiliency and encourage coping skills.

ACTIVITY
1. Distribute the handouts and pens.
2. Ask a group member to read the top boxed paragraphs, with passion.
3. Give group members fifteen minutes to complete the handout.
4. Divide group into pairs.
5. Give them ten minutes to compare notes and share.
6. Reconvene and ask each group member to share one inspiration or thought from his or her partner.

VARIATIONS
1) Bring poetry or quotations relevant to this topic and read before or after the session.
2) In large print on a banner or poster board, write the last question of the handout along with all of the comments from the group members. Post it where staff or younger people might benefit from this collective wisdom.

NOTES

Topic III
EMOTIONAL EXPRESSION
Table of Contents and Corresponding Goals for Each Section

> *Unexpressed emotions will never die.*
> *They are buried alive and will come forth later in uglier ways.*
> ~ Sigmund Freud

Talk About Feelings.. 35
To facilitate healthy conversations about feelings.
To recognize the benefits of expressing feelings.

Effects of Emotional Abuse.. 37
To identify some of the effects one suffers from emotional abuse.

If I Could Write a Book About My Life....................... 39
To increase emotional expression and disclosure.
To increase life satisfaction by reviewing personal stories.

My Rights as a Senior Adult...................................... 41
To address the emotional needs and rights of a senior adult.

Reveal How You Feel.. 43
To uncover and share one's true feelings.

LEVEL OF UNDERSTANDING

 Basic Level    Intermediate Level    High Level

Topic III — EMOTIONAL EXPRESSION

Talk About Feelings

Afraid	Angry	Bored	Confident	Confused
Crabby	Depressed	Determined	Disappointed	Discouraged
Embarrassed	Excited	Frustrated	Glad	Grateful
Guilty	Helpless	Hopeful	Hurt	Interested
Jealous	Lonely	Loved	Nervous	Optimistic
Overwhelmed	Peaceful	Proud	Regretful	Relieved
Satisfied	Suspicious	Thoughtful	Tired	Withdrawn

OPTIMAL WELL-BEING FOR SENIOR ADULTS I

Talk About Feelings
Leader's Guide

PURPOSE
To facilitate healthy conversations about feelings.

To recognize the benefits of expressing feelings.

POSSIBLE NAMES OF SESSIONS
- *Speaking the Unspoken … EMOTIONS!*
- *Feelings For a Lifetime*
- *Better Out Than In!*

BACKGROUND INFORMATION
Expressing our feelings can be quite a challenge! To know what we are feeling and then to be able to find the right words to express it to others is a lifelong skill. Oftentimes we live life with feelings stirring below the surface but can't find the language. The thirty-five words listed on this handout are commonly felt but are often unexpressed.

ACTIVITY
1. Write on the board, "How Are You Feeling?"
2. Ask group members to name what they typically hear as a response: "fine," "OK," "good."
3. Explain that this session focuses on expanding the vocabulary and the skill of identifying feelings.
4. Ask group members about the multitude of consequences or implications of NOT expressing one's feelings, e.g., impaired relationships, risky behaviors, etc. Consider relevant answers exploring the mind-body connection.
5. Distribute handouts and pens.
6. Explain that emotions rarely come one at a time. We often feel several emotions simultaneously. Emotions are not negative or positive; instead they can be viewed as comfortable and uncomfortable. Expressing uncomfortable feelings may be difficult, but will lead to a healthier lifestyle and growth.
7. Ask each group member to circle one comfortable feeling and one uncomfortable feeling experienced in the last few days.
8. Give everyone an opportunity to express the comfortable emotion in a structured, simple format:
   "I feel _____ when _____."
   For example, "I feel relieved when the doctor gives me a clean bill of health."
   "I felt _____ when _____."
   For example, "I felt satisfied when I was enjoying time with my grandchildren yesterday."
9. Then do the same with uncomfortable emotions.
   For example, "I feel helpless when I try to move quickly in the morning and can't."
   For example, "I felt jealous when I went to Sally's house and saw her so happy with her family."
10. Encourage group members to post the handout in a visible place where it can be referred to easily.

VARIATIONS
1) Explore a possible relationship between early messages received about emotional expression by the people who raised us, and how we express emotions today.
2) Create a *How I Feel Today* collage with magazine cutouts, using the handout as a guide.
3) Brainstorm *feelings* words that come to mind that are NOT listed on the handout. (*Ex: betrayed*)

Topic III — EMOTIONAL EXPRESSION

Effects of Emotional Abuse

The words in this search are all possible effects of emotional abuse.
The words can be found forward, backward, upward, downward, diagonal, or backwards diagonal.

Y	S	E	S	U	B	A	E	C	N	A	T	S	B	U	S
H	S	T	D	D	E	S	T	R	U	C	T	I	V	E	A
T	R	H	R	R	S	R	E	J	E	C	T	I	O	N	D
S	E	N	Y	E	S	E	W	L	S	S	R	E	C	L	U
U	D	O	O	J	I	D	M	U	I	P	E	U	O	O	M
R	R	V	S	P	V	R	A	A	V	C	N	B	M	W	R
T	O	A	I	G	A	O	K	C	L	W	W	Y	P	S	L
F	S	L	G	A	W	S	U	L	O	B	T	W	U	E	E
O	I	U	D	E	I	I	S	R	E	L	N	C	L	L	R
K	D	E	A	N	A	D	T	I	I	U	D	E	S	F	U
C	P	K	E	B	F	H	C	U	V	S	F	G	I	E	C
A	E	D	S	C	V	C	G	P	B	E	I	H	V	S	E
L	E	E	S	L	O	E	R	U	L	I	A	F	E	T	S
K	L	A	T	F	L	E	S	E	V	I	T	A	G	E	N
P	S	E	S	W	O	P	O	M	A	E	J	G	N	E	I
R	D	E	P	R	E	S	S	E	D	M	R	J	O	M	K

BLAMES
COLD
COMPULSIVE
DEPRESSED
DESTRUCTIVE
FAILURE

GUILTY
INSECURE
LACK OF TRUST
LOW SELF ESTEEM
NEGATIVE SELF TALK
NO VALUE

PASSIVE
RAGE
REJECTION
SHY
SLEEP DISORDERS
SPEECH DISORDERS

SUBSTANCE ABUSE
ULCERS
UNWORTHY
WEAK

OPTIMAL WELL-BEING FOR SENIOR ADULTS I

Effects of Emotional Abuse
Leader's Guide

PURPOSE
To identify some of the effects one suffers from emotional abuse.

POSSIBLE NAMES OF SESSIONS
- *Searching for the Truth About Emotional Abuse*
- *The Aftermath of Emotional Abuse*
- *What is Emotional Abuse, Anyway?*

BACKGROUND INFORMATION
Too often people are unaware of the toll that emotional abuse places on their lives. This activity is meant to bring to light some of the effects of emotional abuse.

VARIATIONS
1) Review explanations listed above as a separate group session.
2) Invite a professional to come to the next session to discuss "What to Do If You are Living in an Emotionally Abusive Situation."
Inform group members that emotionally abusive relationships might include parent-child, grandparent-grandchild, partners, landlord-tenant, or other combinations.

ACTIVITY
1. Define emotional abuse: Any act, including confinement, isolation, verbal assault, humiliation, intimidation, or any other treatment which may diminish one's sense of self-identity and self-worth.
2. Explain that people who have been abused repeatedly report that out of all forms of abuse, emotional abuse is the most difficult to overcome.
3. Distribute handouts, highlighters and pens.
4. Give participants ample time to complete the word search.
5. Discuss by using explanations below. Give examples of how each effect could be a result of emotional abuse.

Blame: People who are abused often blame themselves because they are accustomed to being blamed by the abuser.

Cold: People who have been emotionally abused can become cold and insensitive to others' feelings because that is how they were treated. They have learned to respond to others in the same way.

Compulsive: Compulsiveness may arise from being exposed to repeated emotional abuse.

Depressed: In an emotionally abusive relationship, depression is common due to the negative, unyielding, and hopeless environment.

Destructive: The pain that people who have been emotionally abused suffer inside can be so intense that they find destructive ways such as self-mutilation, substances, or suicide attempts to try and rid themselves of the pain.

Failure: People who have been emotionally abused have been told in words and/or actions, that they are worthless. This can make them feel as if they cannot succeed.

Guilty: People who have experienced emotional abuse can feel that the abuse is their fault and feel guilty for "provoking" the abuser.

Insecure: People who have been abused often find that they don't have a 'safe-place' to vent feelings and share concerns. They do not feel secure in the world.

Lack of Trust: People who have experienced emotional abuse can become distrustful of those around them because they do not know if and when the abuser will 'explode' and when they will become the target of aggression.

Low Self-Esteem: After repeatedly hearing negative comments, self-esteem becomes diminished.

Negative Self-Talk: When people repeatedly hear devaluing comments, they start to believe them and perpetuate the abuse by putting themselves down.

No Value: People who have experienced emotional abuse often feel as if they are undeserving and have no value.

Passive: People who have been emotionally abused often learn to be submissive to the abuse and are afraid to stand up for their rights.

Rage: Rage can build up inside of those abused because they feel angry about what is or has happened to them.

Rejection: People who have been abused will reject any positive comment or compliment because they do not feel worthy.

Shy: People who have experienced emotional abuse may feel shy or timid around people for several reasons such as low self-worth, feeling undeserving of friendships, and afraid that others may find out how things operate in their homes.

Sleep Disorders: Nightmares, sleep disturbances, etc., are often a result of emotional abuse.

Speech Disorders: Emotional abuse takes its toll on the brain and can result in speech disorders.

Substance Abuse: To escape from the pain from emotional abuse, many people turn to drugs or alcohol to help them escape temporarily from the reality that they are facing.

Ulcers: Emotional abuse results in stress induced ulcers or other physical issues.

Unworthy: People who have experienced emotional abuse often feel unworthy of love or attention from others due to the pattern of interaction they have or had with the perpetrator.

Weak: People who have experienced emotional abuse can feel weak and feel they have no control, particularly around the abuser.

Topic III — EMOTIONAL EXPRESSION

If I Could Write a Book About My Life

It would begin with …

The easiest chapter for me to write would be …

I would leave out the part about …

The most difficult chapter for me to write would be …

I would let _____ read it.
(specify: anyone, a certain person, no one)

I *would / would not* include information about all of my family members. (*circle would or would not*)

One person I would highlight is …

The most interesting chapter would be …

The chapter people would have a hard time believing is …

The chapter that would surprise people most would be …

I would dedicate my book to …

A possible title for my book might be …

OPTIMAL WELL-BEING FOR SENIOR ADULTS I

If I Could Write a Book About My Life
Leader's Guide

PURPOSE
To increase emotional expression and disclosure.

To increase life satisfaction by reviewing personal stories.

POSSIBLE NAMES OF SESSIONS
- *Telling My Story*
- *My Book*
- *Xtra, Xtra, Read All About It*

BACKGROUND INFORMATION
The ability to self-disclose has a direct effect on an individual's potential for recovery and self-discovery. Using incomplete sentence stems or starters facilitates such disclosure, while at the same time incorporating an activity that condenses a person's life story. This creative alternative to verbal emotional expression can easily be a launching pad to lively verbal expression.

ACTIVITY
1. Begin by discussing the writing of one's memoirs. Remind each group member that although only a small percentage of people actually write a book about themselves – everyone's life story is interesting, unique, and worth telling.
2. Distribute handouts and pens.
3. Encourage group members to complete the sentence stems. Explain that there are no right or better responses, only different ones, since each person in the group is a special person with a story to tell.
4. Elicit responses from group members:
   a) Ask each sentence stem at a time of each person.
   b) Or, have each participant respond to all of the sentence stems on the handout at one time.
5. Expound on specific sentence stems. Explore reasons for what each group member would delete (if any), why a certain chapter would be more difficult to write, or the meaning behind the individual titles of books. Group facilitator can expound on any sentence stem.
6. Discuss with group the value of writing memoirs: *"If it's not written down, it will be lost." "Each person has a story to tell." "No one has a journey just like yours." "Your story matters."*
7. Encourage group members to start on their memoirs.

VARIATIONS
1) Talk about benefits of journaling, e.g., as a way to relieve tension, having a listener who is always available, using an alternative means of emotional expression, exploring a way of healing. Discuss the various forms of journaling. Determine who has kept a journal or diary in the past, why they stopped, who is considering keeping one again, or starting one for the first time. Remind members that they do not need to tell their life story. They can take one day at a time to express their thoughts and emotions.
2) Create new sentence stems with group members, write them on the board and give everyone an opportunity to respond. Examples: *My thank you page would include _____. The cover of my book would look like _____.*

NOTES
_____
_____
_____
_____

Topic III — EMOTIONAL EXPRESSION

My Rights as a Senior Adult

***I would like to ask for the following courtesies:
allow me to live with the utmost honor, dignity, and respect.***

Check the following as they apply to you, and add details in your own words on the blank lines.

☐ 1. Talk to me as a capable adult and make sure you are aware of my wants and needs. _____
_____

☐ 2. I want to feel as if I can do certain productive things. Give me opportunities. _____
_____

☐ 3. I want to hear you. Talk loudly without screaming or talking too slowly, so I won't need to ask you to repeat. _____
_____

☐ 4. Be patient with me. _____
_____

☐ 5. My sense of humor is still here. Have fun with me! _____
_____

☐ 6. Make sense of what I am saying by giving me extra time and by asking me good questions. _____
_____

☐ 7. Be present when you're with me. Really listen. _____
_____

☐ 8. Focus on my strengths and de-emphasize my limitations and shortcomings that I can't do anything about. _____
_____

☐ 9. Touch me physically in a safe and loving way. _____
_____

☐ 10. Support me in enjoying satisfying and healthy relationships and do not let me be subjected to physical, sexual, financial, verbal, or emotional abuse. _____
_____

☐ Other _____
_____

☐ Other _____
_____

OPTIMAL WELL-BEING FOR SENIOR ADULTS I

My Rights as a Senior Adult
Leader's Guide

PURPOSE
To address the emotional needs and rights of a senior adult.

POSSIBLE NAMES OF SESSIONS
- *This is What I Need*
- *Tough Things To Talk About?*
- *I Have Rights!*

BACKGROUND INFORMATION
This handout assertively states a "What I need from you" approach. Being a senior adult isn't always easy. The senior adults' specific needs and rights are sometimes overlooked. Considering these needs will enhance communication, healthy interactions, and promote positive, supportive relationships.

ACTIVITY
1. Explain background information.
2. Distribute handouts and pens.
3. Discuss each item, allowing group members to raise concerns about specific rights.
4. Instruct group members to check the boxes of the 'rights,' and add in their own comments on the lines below each one that relates to them personally.
5. Allow for further ideas to be shared on the 'Others' at the bottom.
6. Divide groups into pairs to allow for problem solving for ways to approach these issues.
   - Is it best to discuss these issues *directly* with the person involved?
   - What are strategies for direct communication of this nature?
   - Is it best to discuss them *indirectly*?
   - If indirectly, what are some methods?

   For example, referring to the front of the handout:
   Number 3. Speaking in a volume you can hear.
   Number 4. Thanking a person who is patient.
7. Reconvene and share results of work shared in pairs.

VARIATIONS
1) Role play one direct and one indirect method of communication with each of the ten 'rights.'
2) Problem solve difficult conversations regarding rights.
   For example: My caregiver frequently says, *"Don't you remember when I told you that?"*

NOTES
_____
_____
_____
_____
_____
_____
_____
_____

Topic III — EMOTIONAL EXPRESSION

Reveal How You Feel

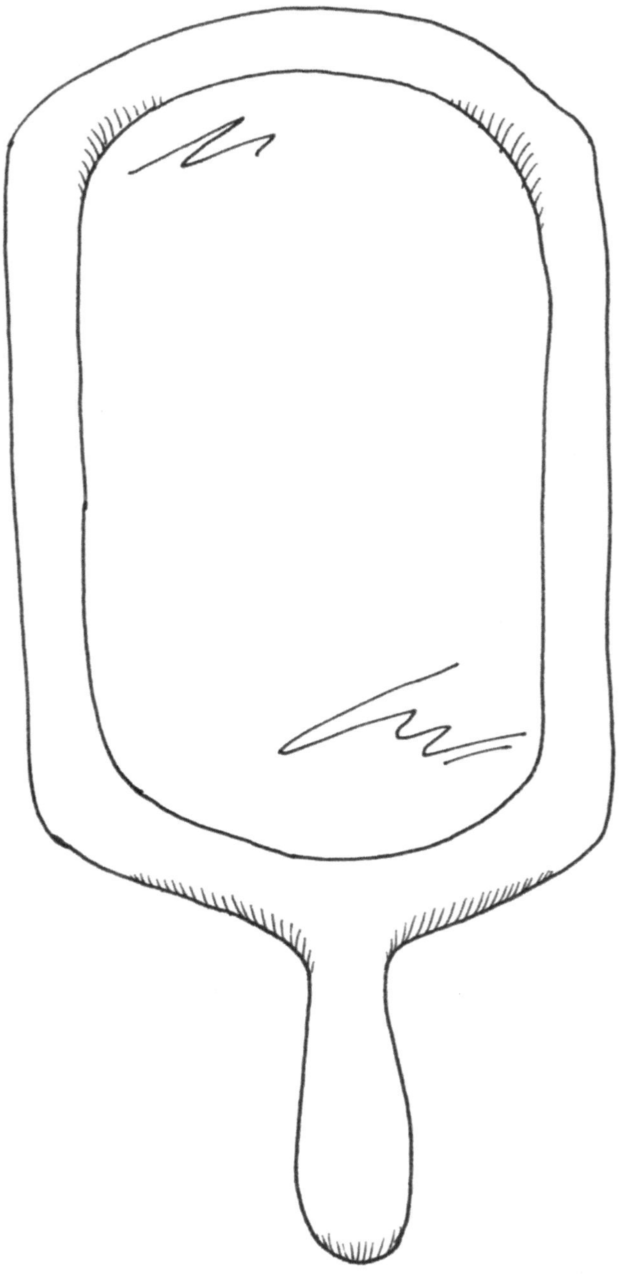

Mirror, Mirror   **Mirror, Mirror**

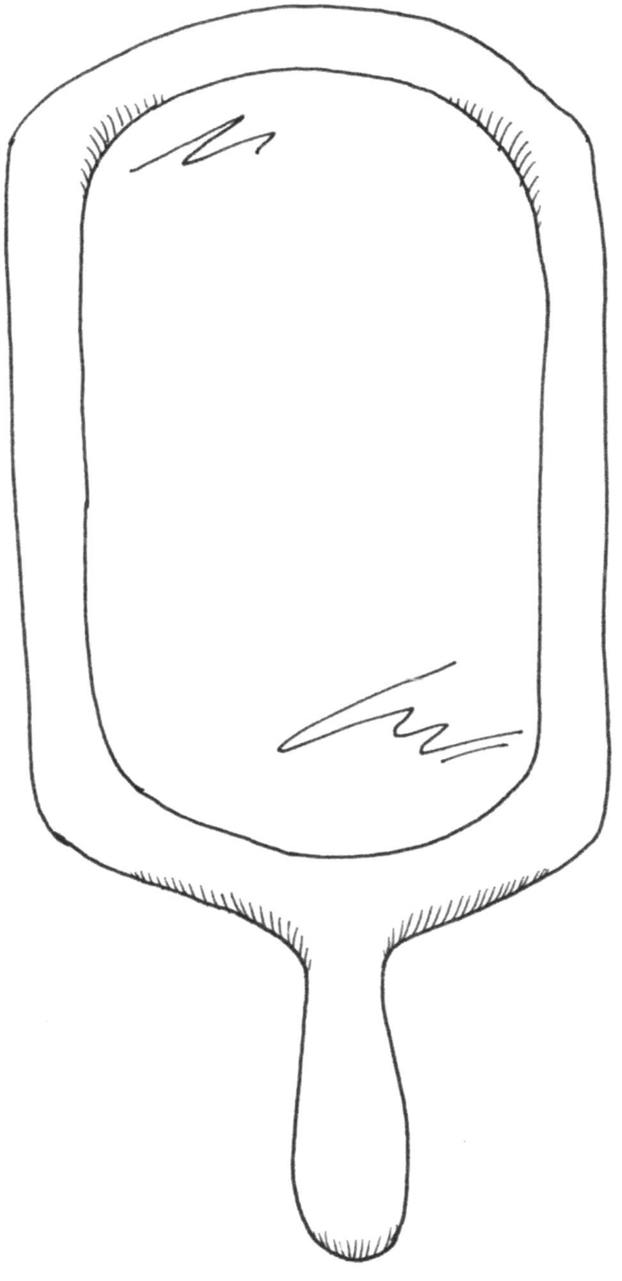

OPTIMAL WELL-BEING FOR SENIOR ADULTS I

Reveal How You Feel
Leader's Guide

PURPOSE

To uncover and share one's true feelings.

POSSIBLE NAMES OF SESSIONS

- *Mirror, Mirror*
- *What's Under the Mask?*
- *Superhero and Me … What Do We Have in Common?*

BACKGROUND INFORMATION

Knowing how we feel and being able to express those true feelings can help us improve the quality of our lives. Too often we wear masks that show others what we think they want to see, or what we want them to see. By pretending false feelings, we are denying ourselves the opportunity to be ourselves, to connect with others, and to make progress.

ACTIVITY

1. Discuss how difficult it is to reveal what's really going on in our lives. Briefly, list a few possible obstacles. *Example: I fear that if people see the real me, they would be scared, they won't like me, and won't think the same of me.*
2. Distribute handouts and markers.
3. In the mirror on the left, ask the group members to draw the mask that they wear for others. Discuss the perceived benefits of wearing these masks. Also discuss the drawbacks.
4. Ask the group members to draw a picture on the right-hand mirror of how they really feel. Discuss what it would be like to have others see or know their true feelings.
5. Ask the group members to give each other feedback regarding the mask vs. the true expression of feelings.
6. Discuss the impact of both masks and true emotional expression.

VARIATIONS

1) Pair group members.
   Give them each a new handout.
   Ask group member A to draw how she sees group member B's handout, in the mirror on the left on her handout.
   Ask group member B to draw how he sees group member A's handout, in the mirror on the left on his handout.
   Then, ask group members to trade papers and draw how they could be seen without a mask in the mirror on the right of their handouts.
2) After both mirrors are finished, gather handouts for everyone to see, and look for similarities and differences. Factors to look for might include gender, ethnic background, age, culture, professions, etc.

NOTES

_____
_____
_____
_____
_____
_____
_____
_____

Topic IV

GRIEF AND LOSS

Table of Contents and Corresponding Goals for Each Section

The reality is that you will grieve forever. You will not 'get over' the loss of a loved one; you will learn to live with it. You will heal and you will rebuild yourself around the loss you suffered. You will be whole again but you will never be the same. Nor should you be the same nor would you want to.

~ Elisabeth Kübler–Ross

Grief Grabs You 47

To facilitate the grief process:
1) Acknowledging often unrecognized symptoms and feelings.
2) Recognize benefits of discussing grief in a group setting.

Grief Feels Like 49

To release feelings surrounding grief issues.
To use visual images of grief to assist in the healing process.

Inside Outside 51

To gain insight regarding the discrepancy between how one feels and what one expresses while experiencing grief.
To identify the implications of the "Inside, I feel ..." and "Outside, I appear ..." discrepancy, and to define ways to bridge the gap of this discrepancy.

Steps of Grief 53

To become aware of possible stages or steps of grief.
To explore the experiences of the different stages or steps of grief.

Healing From A Loss 55

To increase awareness of feelings regarding a loss and feelings associated with the expression of healing.
To identify triggers (or stressors) that affect reactions to loss.
To identify sources of comfort in the healing process following a death or loss.

LEVEL OF UNDERSTANDING

Basic Level | Intermediate Level | High Level

Topic IV — GRIEF AND LOSS

Grief Grabs You
when you're least prepared!

Do you ...
☐ Cry for no reason at all?
☐ Feel a tug at your heart when you see a striking resemblance, a familiar hairdo, certain clothing?
☐ Feel angry at a loved one you lost, yourself, your family, or people who are trying to help you?
☐ Feel cheated?
☐ Feel fine for a period of time, and then feel depressed for no apparent reason?
☐ Feel like no one really understands the depth of your loss and sadness?
☐ Feel lonely even though you are in a room filled with people?
☐ Feel overwhelmed with the flooding of many emotions?
☐ Find it hard to imagine that others' lives go on? That people are still laughing? That the sun still shines?
☐ Forget what you were about to do five minutes ago?
☐ Have a difficult time concentrating?
☐ Have a sense of being incomplete?
☐ Try to sleep but think too much?
☐ Want to stay in bed, or better yet, climb under the bed?
☐ Wish your loved one who is no longer in your life, could see your children, see what you are accomplishing, etc.?
☐ Other _____
☐ Other _____
☐ Other _____
☐ Other _____
☐ Other _____

Do you feel saddened when ...
☐ It's the anniversary date of a birthday? Wedding? Death? Divorce?
☐ You go to a religious or spiritual ceremony or service? Meaningful event?
☐ You hear a certain song? Certain type of music?
☐ You see a couple arm-in-arm?
☐ You see a parent and child, siblings, best friends, etc. together?
☐ You see people happy and carefree, and not mourning your loss?
☐ You see the beauty of everything blooming in spring? The leaves turning color in fall?
☐ You smell a familiar cologne, shaving lotion, etc.?
☐ Other _____
☐ Other _____
☐ Other _____
☐ Other _____
☐ Other _____

Grief Grabs You
Leader's Guide

PURPOSE
To facilitate the grief process:
1) Acknowledging often unrecognized symptoms and feelings.
2) Recognize benefits of discussing grief in a group setting.

POSSIBLE NAMES OF SESSIONS
- *Dealing with Grief in a Group*
- *My Grief … Your Grief*
- *Feeling My Grief? Not ME!*

BACKGROUND INFORMATION
Grief is an intense feeling of deep sorrow and sadness caused by a loss. Oftentimes when people are experiencing grief symptoms, they feel alone, isolated and unsupported. It is important for people who are grieving to realize that they are not alone and that others have experienced similar grief symptoms and feelings.

ACTIVITY
1. Present concept of grief 'grabbing' people when they least expect it.
2. Distribute handouts and pens. Ask group members to complete them and then share what they wrote.
3. Discuss each situation and ask for volunteers to share their experiences.
4. Pursue "Other" comments on the bottom of each list. Ask members if they have noticed a difference as time has passed.
5. Process the benefits of recognizing grief symptoms and feelings, and of discussing grief in a group setting vs. grieving alone.

VARIATIONS
1) Discuss each situation listed on the handout, and ask a group member to volunteer to share an emotion that co-exists with grief in that particular situation. Assist group members by using a list of varied emotions. See *Talk About Feelings*, Page 35.
2) Write 'What Has Helped' on the board. Ask group members to name those things that have helped in the grief process and list them on the board. List may include: people listening to me, getting a good night's sleep, talking to others who have lost someone, being outdoors.
3) Read the following quotation by Elisabeth Kübler-Ross to the group and then have a group discussion about it.
   The reality is that you will grieve forever. You will not "get over" the loss of a loved one; you will learn to live with it. You will heal and you will rebuild yourself around the loss you have suffered. You will be whole again, but you will never be the same. Nor should you be the same nor would you want to.

NOTES
_____
_____
_____
_____
_____
_____
_____
_____

Topic IV — GRIEF AND LOSS

Grief Feels Like

A Puzzle

A Broken Heart

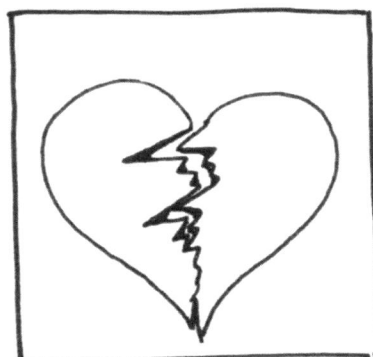

Missing Pieces or Wounds

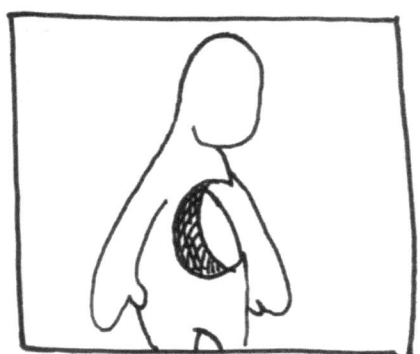

Waves

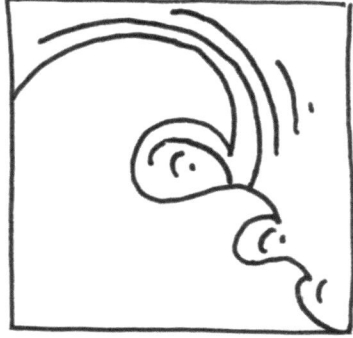

A Rapid River

A Maze

An Illness

Your Drawing

Your Drawing

Grief Feels Like
Leader's Guide

PURPOSE
To release feelings surrounding grief issues.

To use visual images of grief to assist in the healing process.

POSSIBLE NAMES OF SESSIONS
- *What Does YOUR Grief Feel Like?*
- *Good Grief*
- *Looking at Grief in a New Way!*

BACKGROUND INFORMATION
Grief is a universal and personal process after a loss. It is also a powerful emotion and is as individual as the person experiencing it. Encouraging group members to creatively imagine how grief feels can help develop a common language and allow for acceptance of feelings. Grieving is a process that can lead to healing and personal growth.

ACTIVITY
1. Allow group members to describe their feelings of grief in their own words.
2. Explain the concept of grief by reviewing the background information.
3. Distribute handouts and thin colored markers.
4. Discuss the imagery of each picture and how grief can feel. Give or elicit an example for each picture, e.g., a wave of emotions or feelings may occur in a car when the radio is on and a certain song is playing and it reminds them of a person, place or situation. Encourage group members to color images as they see fit.
5. Ask individuals to draw in their own image of what grief feels like to them in the last two boxes and share.
6. Ask group members to circle the image that they feel best reflects their personal grief process.
7. Process benefits of this activity.

VARIATIONS
1) After completion of activity above, ask group members to write a short story about their grief and how it feels to them, or how they perceive it to be. Ask them to include images discussed and coping skills they have used or would like to use.
2) Gather magazines and ask members to cut out pictures of what grief feels like. Create a group collage together titled "Grief feels like …" and post it for clients, staff, and families to see.

NOTES
_____
_____
_____
_____
_____
_____
_____
_____
_____

Topic IV — GRIEF AND LOSS

Inside Outside

Describe a specific situation in which you experience grief, e.g., loss of a person, pet, ability.

_____
_____
_____

"Inside, I feel …" (only I know that I am feeling …)	"Outside, I appear …" (other people view me as …)
☐ Angry ☐ Confident ☐ Confused ☐ Crabby ☐ Depressed ☐ Determined ☐ Disappointed ☐ Glad ☐ Grateful ☐ Guilty ☐ Helpless ☐ Hopeful ☐ Hurt ☐ Interested ☐ Lonely ☐ Loved ☐ Peaceful ☐ Relieved ☐ Satisfied ☐ Withdrawn	☐ Angry ☐ Confident ☐ Confused ☐ Crabby ☐ Depressed ☐ Determined ☐ Disappointed ☐ Glad ☐ Grateful ☐ Guilty ☐ Helpless ☐ Hopeful ☐ Hurt ☐ Interested ☐ Lonely ☐ Loved ☐ Peaceful ☐ Relieved ☐ Satisfied ☐ Withdrawn

Implications of Inside / Outside Discrepancy

Physical Symptoms _____
_____
_____
_____

Relationships _____
_____
_____
_____

While it is okay to have some discrepancies between our feelings and expressions, it is also important to recognize that the greater this discrepancy, the greater the internal stress level. Bridging the gap between inside and outside can be done in several ways.

What are some of your ideas? Write them on the back of this paper.

Inside Outside
Leader's Guide

PURPOSE
To gain insight regarding the discrepancy between how one feels and what one expresses while experiencing grief.

To identify the implications of the "Inside, I feel …" and "Outside, I appear …" discrepancy, and to define ways to bridge the gap of this discrepancy.

POSSIBLE NAMES OF SESSIONS
- *It's What I'm Not Telling You!*
- *Grief … Gets In The Way*
- *It's All a Mask!*

BACKGROUND INFORMATION
Oftentimes, people who are grieving feel that no one understands them. They probably do not understand themselves. It might be due to discrepancies between emotion identification and emotion expression. It is vital to remind people that the greater the discrepancy, the greater the internal stress level.
Further implications might involve physical problems or relationship issues, e.g.,
a) Headaches, stomach problems, anxiety attacks, increase in blood pressure.
b) Feelings that other people don't understand, and therefore get the wrong impression.
c) An increase in arguments and irritability.

ACTIVITY
1. Explain the concept of "Inside, I feel …" and "Outside, I appear …" using the following example.

Name a situation	Inside	Outside	Implications
Anniversary of a loved one's death.	☒ *confused* ☒ *lonely* ☒ *hurt* ☒ *depressed*	☒ *peaceful*	*Back pain, feel alone, unsupported and not able to relate to friends.*

2. Distribute handouts and pens, and instruct group members to complete the handout.
3. Ask group members to share with emphasis on implications and ways to bridge the gap of this discrepancy.
4. Process the activity.

VARIATIONS
1) Facilitate role plays by encouraging group members to choose situations in which they were unable to express their grief well. For example: *It was the anniversary of a loved one's death and I was at work. I became angry with my boss when she asked me to do something and then I started an argument with my co-worker.* Encourage group members to first act out the role play as the situation happened, and then work on how to communicate their grief more effectively. Ask members to provide support and feedback for those who are role playing.
2) Make a deck of 20 index cards using the emotions listed on the handout. Ask the group members to choose a card and give an example of when they felt this way during the grief process.

NOTES
_____
_____
_____
_____
_____
_____
_____
_____
_____

Topic IV — GRIEF AND LOSS

Steps of Grief

We go through steps (stages) of grief after a loss.

Many lists describe stages of grief. One list:

SHOCK → SORROW → DENIAL → ANGER → GUILT → DEPRESSION → ACCEPTANCE

Not all persons experience all of these stages of loss.
Stages may be repeated.
No stage lasts indefinitely.
Your stages may not be in this particular order.
All stages are normal.

Keep In Mind That:

Choose one of your losses and write it here: _____

_____

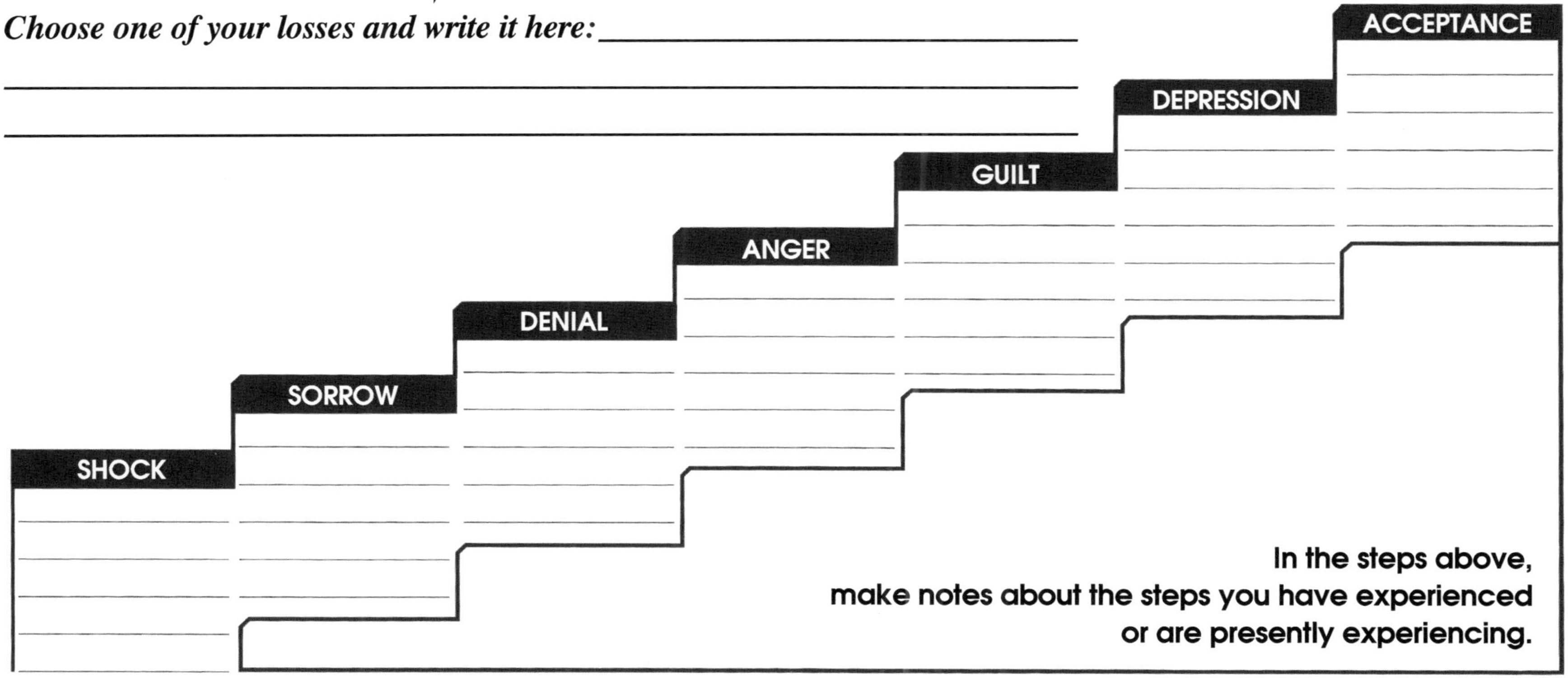

Steps (ascending): SHOCK, SORROW, DENIAL, ANGER, GUILT, DEPRESSION, ACCEPTANCE

In the steps above, make notes about the steps you have experienced or are presently experiencing.

© 2016 WHOLE PERSON ASSOCIATES, 101 WEST 2ND STREET, SUITE 203, DULUTH MN 55802 • 800-247-6789 • WHOLEPERSON.COM

OPTIMAL WELL-BEING FOR SENIOR ADULTS I

Steps of Grief
Leader's Guide

PURPOSE

To become aware of possible stages or steps of grief.

To explore the experiences of the different stages or steps of grief.

POSSIBLE NAMES OF SESSIONS

- *Denial, Shock, Anger … Sound Familiar?*
- *Where Am I in the Stages of Grief?*
- *Stages of Grief … No Surprise!*

BACKGROUND INFORMATION

Everyone goes through stages (steps) of grief after a loss. All people do not necessarily go through all of the stages. Experiences at different stages may vary greatly, causing individuals to feel "weird," "different," and in some cases, as if they are "going crazy." Identifying these stages and feelings, sharing them with others, and knowing others have experienced them can help individuals to understand their own personal journey through grief and feel supported in this process.

ACTIVITY

1. Review concepts as outlined in the Purpose and Background Information.
2. Ask group members to help (if appropriate), to put the names of the seven possible stages (steps) on the floor, using index cards. Seven chairs with signs could be substituted. If space is not available, identified lines could be drawn on a dry-erase board.
3. Instruct people to identify a personal loss and then locate, depending on the activity used, which stage they are in at this moment. In some groups, this may be sitting on the corresponding chair, finding a place on the floor or pointing at a location on the board.
4. Distribute handouts and pencils and instruct group members to complete the page.
5. Share responses in a supportive atmosphere.
6. Review the "Keep in Mind That" section, emphasizing these important points.

VARIATIONS

1) Facilitate discussion and encourage group members to engage in the following:
   a. Share stages of grief that people have experienced.
   b. Help each other with these by saying, "it was helpful for me at that stage when I _____."
   c. As a group, read aloud the "Keep In Mind That" italicized section.
2) Divide group into pairs.
   Allow five minutes for individuals to share their stages:
   a. Least comfortable stage
   b. Most comfortable stage
   c. Present stage

NOTES

_____
_____
_____
_____
_____
_____

Topic IV — GRIEF AND LOSS

Healing From A Loss

Grief or Loss

Healing

Healing From A Loss
Leader's Guide

PURPOSE

To increase awareness of feelings regarding a loss and feelings associated with the expression of healing.

To identify triggers (or stressors) that affect reactions to loss.

To identify sources of comfort in the healing process following a death or loss.

POSSIBLE NAMES OF SESSIONS

- *Time for Healing*
- *Grief Work Begins Now*
- *Expressing Grief … in a Different Way*

BACKGROUND INFORMATION

Each person has had an experience with loss as a source of stress. Grief and loss occur in stages. It is important to recognize and explore methods for reducing the stress associated with the feelings that occur after a loss when healing begins to take place.

ACTIVITY

1. Introduce the topic of grief and the fact that it is universal. Explain that grief results from the pain of loss, a death, job change, disappointments, disruptions in the family, altered friendships, unfulfilled dreams, or diminishing abilities.
2. Elicit examples from group members.
3. Briefly, discuss the topic of imagery and relaxation to assist in grief work.
4. Distribute handouts instructing participants to fold the handout in half. Emphasize that they do not need to have artistic talent to express themselves by drawing.
5. Place a variety of coloring supplies (paint, markers, crayons, colored pencils) in the center of the table, instructing group members to select materials to use for this activity. Create a relaxed, quiet atmosphere during the art expression part of the activity. Playing soft music may assist.
6. Allow ten minutes for the next part of the activity. Instruct group members to close their eyes and think of an image associated with the words "grief" or "loss" and then open their eyes and draw a symbol on the top section of the paper. Ask group members to write words at the bottom of the grief or loss box to describe the image or that may be significant of the image.
7. Allow another ten minutes for the next part of the activity. Direct participants to close their eyes and think of an image associated with "healing" and then open their eyes and draw a symbol on the bottom section of the paper. Then, at the bottom of the healing box, instruct participants to write words to describe the image or that might be significant of the image.
8. Ask for volunteers who wish to share.
9. Ask: What are your reactions to your own creative expression? Emphasize the process and not the product, discouraging comparisons of quality differences between group members.
10. Process by exploring feelings that emerge in the expression of grief and healing (denial, depressions, hope, strength, wisdom, etc.)
11. Encourage other healing and creative opportunities stemming from the grief work (poetry, journaling, artwork, collages, music, etc.).

VARIATIONS

1) Ask participants to relax, guiding them through a deep breathing exercise for several minutes before or after the creative expression activity.
2) Ask participants to describe their personal patterns for managing grief or loss. Are there others in the group with similar patterns? Themes? What are healthy healing hints, strategies, or sources of comfort?

Topic V

LIFE BALANCE
Table of Contents and Corresponding Goals for Each Section

*Life is like riding a bicycle. To keep your balance,
you must keep moving.*

~ Albert Einstein

Find the Balance for Next Week............ 59
To identify tasks to do for the week.
To identify leisure/social activities to do for the week.
To organize one's time better.

Keeping on Schedule............ 61
To offer an organizational tool to ensure that meaningful activities happen when they are scheduled.

Turn The Da_ _ TV Off!............ 63
To recognize the pattern of excessive TV watching.
To identify healthy alternatives to improve life balance.

What is One More Thing?............ 65
To create awareness of the important concept that life balance is comprised of three distinct areas: work, self-care, and leisure.
To identify one activity in each of the three categories of work, self-care, and leisure, to improve overall life balance.

Weekly Schedule............ 67
To establish a desired, written schedule incorporating work (not necessarily employment), self-care, and leisure.

LEVEL OF UNDERSTANDING

Basic Level | Intermediate Level | High Level

Topic V — LIFE BALANCE

Find the Balance for Next Week

Check ✓ the activities you wish to accomplish in the next week and add in your own, in both categories, making sure you have checked the exact same amount in both categories.

RESPONSIBILITIES

- ☐ Banking
- ☐ Cleaning up
- ☐ Doctor appointments
- ☐ Errands
- ☐ Grocery shopping
- ☐ Laundry
- ☐ Paying bills
- ☐ Shopping
- ☐ _____
- ☐ _____
- ☐ _____
- ☐ _____
- ☐ _____
- ☐ _____
- ☐ _____
- ☐ _____
- ☐ _____
- ☐ _____
- ☐ _____
- ☐ _____
- ☐ _____
- ☐ _____

LEISURE & SOCIAL

- ☐ Computer
- ☐ Exercise
- ☐ Go to a movie
- ☐ Listen to music
- ☐ Play cards and/or games
- ☐ Read
- ☐ Visit family
- ☐ Visit friends
- ☐ _____
- ☐ _____
- ☐ _____
- ☐ _____
- ☐ _____
- ☐ _____
- ☐ _____
- ☐ _____
- ☐ _____
- ☐ _____
- ☐ _____
- ☐ _____
- ☐ _____
- ☐ _____

OPTIMAL WELL-BEING FOR SENIOR ADULTS I

Find the Balance for Next Week
Leader's Guide

PURPOSE

To identify tasks to do for the week.

To identify leisure/social activities to do for the week.

To organize one's time better.

POSSIBLE NAMES OF SESSIONS

- *Balancing Responsibilities with FUN!*
- *How Can I Fit It All In?*
- *Planning for Success*

BACKGROUND INFORMATION

Part of being a healthy person is the ability to structure and plan one's week and to organize one's time with well-balanced activities. This handout assists people in identifying what they need and want to accomplish for the week.

ACTIVITY

1. Discuss the benefits of planning one's weekly responsibilities and leisure. The group may develop a list.
2. On a dry erase board, have the group devise a list of possible tasks, chores, and responsibilities. Discuss the importance of doing these things, e.g., keeping the home organized, not letting things build up which can be stressful, having clean clothes, etc.
3. Next, list possible leisure and social activities. Discuss the importance of engaging in leisure and social activities, e.g., enjoying others' company, having a support system, being an interesting person, laughing, etc. Emphasize the need for balance.
4. Distribute handouts and pens.
5. Give ample time to complete the handout. Share results. Discuss challenges and how to overcome obstacles.
6. Discuss where this list can be placed to be easily reviewed.

VARIATIONS

1) Use this activity on Monday mornings and repeat for several weeks to help group members become accustomed to planning their weeks. After the first time, this handout can be used as a warm-up or starter activity for a group session.
2) Encourage group members to write the day of the week for each chosen task/activity.
(M=Monday, TU=Tuesday, W=Wednesday, TH=Thursday, F=Friday, SA=Saturday, SU=Sunday)
3) Use this handout prior to discharge to assist group members in planning ahead.

NOTES

_____
_____
_____
_____
_____
_____
_____
_____

Keeping on Schedule

What I Need To Do	Sunday	Monday	Tuesday	Wednesday	Thursday	Friday	Saturday

What I Need To Do	Sunday	Monday	Tuesday	Wednesday	Thursday	Friday	Saturday

What I Need To Do	Sunday	Monday	Tuesday	Wednesday	Thursday	Friday	Saturday

What I Need To Do	Sunday	Monday	Tuesday	Wednesday	Thursday	Friday	Saturday

Topic V — LIFE BALANCE

Keeping on Schedule
Leader's Guide

PURPOSE
To offer an organizational tool to ensure that meaningful activities happen when they are scheduled.

POSSIBLE NAMES OF SESSIONS
- *Making Sure It Happens*
- *What To Do First?*
- *Organizing My Life … so no one else needs to!!!*

BACKGROUND INFORMATION
Responsibilities can easily be overwhelming to all of us as we plan: appointments; exercise programs; vitamins and medications; phone calls; home maintenance; activities with children; grandchildren and friends; paying bills, etc. It can become burdensome and stressful just thinking about everything. Checklists serve as a way to organize information and are a way of setting up a self-accountability schedule.

ACTIVITY
1. Distribute one handout and a pencil to each group member.
2. List on the board all of the things that group members do in a day. This list may include medications (over-the-counter or prescriptions), vitamins, exercises, appointments, telephone calls, visits, health care activities (taking blood pressure, listening to relaxation tapes) and meetings.
3. Check off <u>only</u> those activities that they have difficulty remembering.
4. Explain that this handout serves as an organizational tool for only those activities.
5. Give group members ten minutes to complete the handout. A few ways to use this handout:
   a. One activity for a month - *example: Take a medication three times a day*. Instruct the group members to place three checks (✔) in each day's box. Once the activity is accomplished, it gets a backwards slash through the check. (✔) Some people might find writing the date below the day of the week helpful.
   b. Use as a weekly guide with non-everyday responsibilities. Instruct group members to write in four activities for the week – *example: call my therapist and ask a question (TU), do my leg exercises (MWF), babysit for grandkids (TU and TH), water the plants SU)*.
   c. Collaborate and develop another system individualized for the people in the session.
6. Ask each person to share the completed handout with the group.
7. Provide additional handouts for future use.

VARIATIONS
1) Before the session, develop a few fictitious checklists to share with the group.
2) Use this handout with other handouts in this workbook that will reinforce follow-through of a needed activity.

NOTES

_____
_____
_____
_____
_____
_____

Topic V — LIFE BALANCE

Turn The Da_ _ TV Off!

Many people identify with this real problem in their lives …

The da_ _ TV is on longer than it should be!

Common answers that explain TV watching:
- *Loneliness*
- *Filling in*
- *Filling in the silence*
- *Company*
- *I have nothing better to do*

Bottom line: Many of us watch too much television!

1. How many hours a day of watching TV is the right amount for you? _____
2. Which show is most important to you? _____
3. What are you most likely to do if you *reallocate your time?* Choose only two.
   - ☐ Clean
   - ☐ Crafts
   - ☐ Exercise
   - ☐ Garden
   - ☐ Meditate
   - ☐ Outdoors
   - ☐ Play games/crosswords
   - ☐ Read
   - ☐ Visit
   - ☐ Walk
   - ☐ Write
   - ☐ Other _____
   - ☐ Other _____

4. What is one benefit you may gain by reducing your television time?

_____

_____

_____

Turn The Da_ _ TV Off!
Leader's Guide

PURPOSE
To recognize the pattern of excessive TV watching.

To identify healthy alternatives to improve life balance.

POSSIBLE NAMES OF SESSIONS
- *Taking Charge of My Time*
- *TV by Default*
- *It's Not So Good for Me*

BACKGROUND INFORMATION
The passive nature of watching television can be detrimental to health. Oftentimes, TV shows negative, disturbing, and mind-numbing situations. They present a distorted view of reality. Purposeful, conscious choices of entertainment is a healthy distinction that can be made and emphasized.

ACTIVITY
1. Discuss concept of television watching and how easy it is to put it on with the remote and keep *flicking* until a show gets one's attention. Present that too much television can lead to health problems: sitting too long, avoiding other healthy activities, and watching disturbing images can prevent sound sleep, etc.
2. Distribute handouts and pens.
3. Encourage group members to complete individually.
4. Share results, problem solve, and support efforts to reduce television time.

VARIATIONS
1) Discuss how easy it is to watch television: the remote, abundance of stations, ability to record shows, variety of shows, 24/7 availability. Ask: *Is this technology helping or hurting our society?*
2) Bring a remote to the session and ask group members (in a kidding manner): *Is THIS your best friend?*
   Draw parallels of how it could be your best friend:
   > It doesn't talk back.
   > It feels good to hold it.
   > It's always charged up and ready to go.
   > It's always there when you need it.
   > It's good to hang out with.
   > It's ready to do an activity with you at any time you choose.
   > It's reliable.
   > It's there when you need it.
3) Adapt this handout, as needed, for other excessive behaviors, e.g., computers and hand-held-games.

NOTES
_____
_____
_____
_____
_____
_____
_____
_____

Topic V — LIFE BALANCE

What is One More Thing?

What is one more thing I can do to improve my overall life balance?

Work
(not necessarily employment)
Something I am serious about
that I can contribute to
and that is meaningful to me …

Self-Care
Some way of taking good care of myself …

LEISURE
Something I can do for re-creating, having fun, relaxing, laughing, and enjoying …

What is One More Thing?
Leader's Guide

PURPOSE
To create awareness of the important concept that life balance is comprised of three distinct areas: work, self-care, and leisure.

To identify one activity in each of the three categories of work, self-care, and leisure to improve overall life balance.

POSSIBLE NAMES OF SESSIONS
- *Life Balance*
- *Work? You Want Me to Work??*
- *It's All About Balance*

BACKGROUND INFORMATION
A wellness concept is that no matter what age we are, there is an internal balance established when each of us is involved in work, self-care, and leisure. (Work in this context is not necessarily employment, but instead, work can be contributing or serving at some level and involves meaningful activity.)

ACTIVITY
1. Distribute handouts and pens.
2. Write WORK, SELF-CARE and LEISURE in three different areas on the dry erase board.
3. Explore each area with examples. Take care to explain that work is NOT necessarily employment. It can include volunteering, caregiving, visiting lonely neighbors, cleaning up litter on the streets, calling sick friends, etc. Explain that there are some activities that can be applied to two or three categories such as hiking and cleaning up litter.
4. Encourage group members to take notes on their handouts and complete the handout by responding to this question: *What is one more thing I can do in this area to improve my overall life balance?*
5. Share responses.

VARIATIONS
1) Either before or after completing the handout, ask group members to rate their recent satisfaction with each area on a scale from 1 (lowest) to 10 (highest). Example: Work 3, self-care 1, leisure 4. Adjust upcoming group topics accordingly.
2) Discuss obstacles to achieve life balance along with creative, realistic problem-solving to address these obstacles.
3) Follow up with the handout "Weekly Schedule", Page 67.

NOTES
_____
_____
_____
_____
_____
_____
_____
_____
_____
_____
_____

Topic V — LIFE BALANCE

Weekly Schedule

Name _____ Month _____ Day _____ Year _____

TIME	SUN.	MON.	TUES.	WED.	THURS.	FRI.	SAT.
6:00 a.m.							
6:30 a.m.							
7:00 a.m.							
7:30 a.m.							
8:00 a.m.							
8:30 a.m.							
9:00 a.m.							
9:30 a.m.							
10:00 a.m.							
10:30 a.m.							
11:00 a.m.							
11:30 a.m.							
12:00 noon							
12:30 p.m.							
1:00 p.m.							
1:30 p.m.							
2:00 p.m.							
2:30 p.m.							
3:00 p.m.							
3:30 p.m.							
4:00 p.m.							
4:30 p.m.							
5:00 p.m.							
5:30 p.m.							
6:00 p.m.							
6:30 p.m.							
7:00 p.m.							
7:30 p.m.							
8:00 p.m.							
8:30 p.m.							
9:00 p.m.							
9:30 p.m.							
10:00 p.m.							
10:30 p.m.							
11:00 p.m.							
11:30 p.m.							
12 midnight							

Weekly Schedule
Leader's Guide

PURPOSE
To establish a desired, written schedule incorporating work (not necessarily employment), self-care and leisure.

POSSIBLE NAMES OF SESSIONS
- *What I Am Really Doing*
- *Be the Balance*
- *Human Being vs. Human Doing*

BACKGROUND INFORMATION
It is difficult to implement a well-balanced schedule incorporating the three desired areas: work, self-care and leisure. Take care to explain that work is NOT necessarily employment. It can include volunteering, care-giving, visiting lonely neighbors, cleaning up litter on the streets, calling sick friends, etc. Explain that there are some activities that can be applied to two or three categories such as hiking and cleaning up litter. Writing activities on a schedule allows a closer examination and proposal for the upcoming lifestyle.

ACTIVITY
1. Ask group members to identify which areas of their lives need more attention: work (not necessarily employment), self-care, or leisure. Then ask group members, *How many hours of television do you actually watch each day?* Followed up with *How many hours of television is right for you?* Continue asking, in the same manner, about sleep if appropriate.
2. Distribute handouts and pens, asking group members to complete a schedule for the next week. Offer ample time to complete and share, ensuring that a balance is established.
3. Emphasize that each area (work, self-care and leisure) is highly valued. Encourage some blank spots to offer needed freedom and choices.

VARIATIONS
1) Distribute this handout as "homework" following the "What is One More Thing" handout, page 65.
2) Try experimenting with use of colored pens for activities, to ensure that most days have all colors in them.
   Example:
   Work – red
   Leisure – blue
   Self-care – green

NOTES
_____
_____
_____
_____
_____
_____
_____
_____
_____
_____

Topic VI

REMINISCENCE

Table of Contents and Corresponding Goals for Each Section

Memory only slumbers - never dies.
~ Thomas Paine

Sing, Sing A Song 71
To recall song titles or lines, tap into memories of bygone times, and share experiences with one another.

I'll Never Forget the Day I 73
To reminisce, tell stories, and listen to others, to promote healthy aging.

Remember These Sayings? 75
To use sayings as a means for discussions of reminiscence, story-telling, and values discussion.

SLOGANS 77
To reminisce using famous slogans as prompts.

Historic Dates 79
To reminisce about historic dates we have as a community and those that we have personally.

LEVEL OF UNDERSTANDING

 Basic Level    Intermediate Level    High Level

Topic VI — REMINISCENCE

Sing, Sing A Song

Fill in the blanks of these song titles or lines.

My _____ Heaven

Pennsylvania _____

Somewhere Over the _____

_____ Choo Choo

Don't Sit Under the _____ Tree

That Old Black _____

Dancing _____ to _____

Loving That _____ of Mine

Me and My _____

_____, the Beautiful

Oh, Danny _____

I Left My Heart in _____ _____

East Side, West Side, _____ _____ _____ _____

_____ Dust

Little _____ Jug

I Dream Of _____ With the Light Brown Hair

Nothing Could Be _____ Than To Be in _____ in The Morning

Sweet _____, My _____

Someone's in the Kitchen With _____

You Are My _____, My Only _____

Dancing in the _____

_____ Eat Oats And _____ Eat Oats And _____ _____ Eat _____

When the _____ Go Marching In

Sentimental _____

You Made Me _____ You

As _____ Goes By

Sing, Sing A Song
Leader's Guide

PURPOSE
To recall song titles or lines, tap into memories of bygone times, and share experiences with one another.

POSSIBLE NAMES OF SESSIONS
- *Hum a Few Bars!*
- *I Remember That!*
- *Oh Yeah, That's IT!*

BACKGROUND INFORMATION
This fun activity can be used as a reminiscence and recall activity. Music oftentimes holds fond memories of the song itself as well as the surrounding times and circumstances.

ACTIVITY
1. Distribute handouts and pens.
2. Play as individuals or in teams by asking group members to fill in the blanks to the best of their abilities.
3. Share responses.
4. Generate discussions of who sang the song, what was happening in the lives of the group members when this song was popular, and if they have other memories associated with the songs.

KEY
My **Blue** Heaven
Pennsylvania **6-5000**
Somewhere Over the **Rainbow**
Chatanooga Choo Choo
Don't Sit Under the **Apple** Tree
That Old Black **Magic**
Dancing **Cheek** to **Cheek**
Loving That **Man** of Mine
Me and My **Shadow**
America, the Beautiful
Oh, Danny **Boy**
I Left My Heart in **San Francisco**
East Side, West Side, **All Around the Town**
Star Dust
Little **Brown** Jug
I Dream of **Jeanie** with the Light Brown Hair
Nothing Could Be **Finer** Than to Be in **Carolina** in the Morning
Sweet **Adeline**, My **Adeline**
Someone's in the Kitchen With **Dinah**
You Are My **Sunshine**, My Only **Sunshine**
Dancing in the **Dark**
Mares Eat Oats and **Does** Eat Oats and **Little Lambs** Eat **Ivy**
When the **Saints** Go Marching In
Sentimental **Journey**
You Made Me **Love** You
As **Time** Goes By

VARIATIONS
Listen to the songs on CD or computer. Ask who knows these songs and if they would be willing to start a sing-along. Have lyrics available after clients have identified each one.

I'll Never Forget the Day I ...

1	was kissed for the first time	or	drove a car for the first time by myself
2	heard about the tooth fairy	or	got a new pet
3	experienced the death of someone close to me	or	heard really bad news
4	was in really big trouble with my parents	or	was in big trouble in school
5	earned my first job	or	could afford _____
6	told a lie and got caught	or	disappointed my _____
7	did something I shouldn't have done	or	was really hurt
8	announced that I had a partner	or	experienced the miracle of _____
9	traveled to _____	or	held a baby for the first time
10	met my in-law family	or	received my first raise
11	got drunk for the first time	or	got sick away from home
12	realized I was a grown up	or	moved into my own place
13	did something that I knew was really stupid	or	came home with a bad grade from school
14	got my own car	or	really embarrassed myself
15	rode a bike for the first time	or	had to tell my family news they wouldn't like

Topic VI — REMINISCENCE

I'll Never Forget the Day I ...
Leader's Guide

PURPOSE
To reminisce, tell stories, and listen to others, to promote healthy aging.

POSSIBLE NAMES OF SESSIONS
- *The Good Ole Days!*
- *Do You Remember?*
- *The Rest of the Story*

BACKGROUND INFORMATION
Recalling memories is a healthy part of aging. It is a healthy activity that helps validate senior adults by having others listen to their memorable life experiences. Storytelling can be touching, moving, and of great value to the storyteller and to the listeners. Listening to others can help us feel connected, alive, and filled with emotions. This activity is designed to be success-oriented and adaptable.

ACTIVITY
1. Arrange chairs in a circle.
2. Explain the importance of being able to remember and being a good listener.
3. Distribute the handouts.
4. Ask the person on your left to begin with number one. This person will choose from the first or the second prompt, and tell a related story.
5. Proceed around the circle, allowing each group member to tell at least one story.
6. For a future session, develop a new list of prompts that weren't included in this list.

VARIATIONS
1) Use as a part of an intergenerational activity.
2) Allow other members of the group to share a story about the second prompt that was not selected.
3) Cut handout to make fifteen strips. Place in a basket and each group member will pick one strip and choose one of the two prompts and tell a story.

NOTES
_____
_____
_____
_____
_____
_____
_____
_____
_____
_____
_____
_____

Remember These Sayings?

Fill in the blanks. (Example: Blood is thicker than w a t e r .)

A bird in the hand is worth two in the __ __ __ __ .

A penny saved is a penny __ __ __ __ __ __ .

A stitch in time saves __ __ __ __ .

Birds of a feather flock __ __ __ __ __ __ __ .

Buyer __ __ __ __ __ __ .

Children should be seen and not __ __ __ __ __ .

Here today, gone __ __ __ __ __ __ __ .

Laughter is the best __ __ __ __ __ __ __ .

Look before you __ __ __ __ .

Never put off for tomorrow what you can do __ __ __ __ __ .

Sink or __ __ __ __ .

Waste not want __ __ __ .

You are what you __ __ __ .

You can catch more flies with honey than __ __ __ __ __ __ .

You can't take it with __ __ __ .

OPTIMAL WELL-BEING FOR SENIOR ADULTS I

Remember These Sayings?
Leader's Guide

PURPOSE
To use sayings as a means of reminiscencing, story-telling, and values discussion.

POSSIBLE NAMES OF SESSIONS
- *My Mom/Dad Said That*
- *The Sages Speak!*
- *Words to the Wise*

BACKGROUND INFORMATION
There might be a lot of wisdom in old sayings. Many memories are also attached to them, as they taught important values during the growing years. They are short, usually easily remembered, and lend themselves well to discussions.

ACTIVITY
1. Write on the board: *Don't cry over spilt milk*.
2. Ask group members to explain what this means.
3. Explain that these sayings are often values-based and were often told to us when we "needed to hear them."
4. Distribute handouts and pens, asking each group member to fill in the blanks.
5. Ask group members to check two or four of their favorite sayings from the past.
6. After handouts are completed, read the first saying, *A bird in the hand is worth two in the* _____, pausing and allowing group members to say the answer aloud.
7. Ask one of the group members who answered correctly to explain the saying, and give a real-life example of how that saying could be applied.
8. Ask all of the group members if the saying is still relevant in their lives.
9. Continue with all of the sayings.
10. Encourage members to disagree with any statement, and provide reasons (e.g. – "Children should be seen and not heard.")

VARIATIONS
1) Develop a new list of sayings or proverbs that were not listed on this activity handout.
2) Play a guessing letter game with the sayings.
   For example: _ _ _ _ _ _ _ _ _ _ _ _ _ _ _ _ _ _ .
   (A watched pot never boils)

NOTES
_____
_____
_____
_____
_____
_____
_____
_____

SLOGANS

**Fill in the blanks of these famous advertising slogans.
Then, write the advertiser, and your best guess of the year the slogan was first used.**

Slogan	Advertiser	Year
A Little _____ Do You		
All the _____ That's Fit to Print		
Betcha Can't Eat Just _____		
Better Things for Better Living, Through _____		
Breakfast of _____		
Don't Leave Home _____ _____		
Finger _____ Good		
Fly the Friendly _____		
Good to the _____ _____		
How Do You Spell _____		
I Can't Believe I ___ the _____ Thing		
I'd Like to Teach the World to _____		
I'd Walk a _____ for a _____		
In the Valley of the _____ _____ _____		
It Takes a Licking and Keeps on _____		
Ivory Soap – It _____		
Leave the _____ to Us		
Like a Good Neighbor, _____ _____ Is There		
Look Ma, No _____		
Melts in Your _____ … Not in Your _____		
Mmmm Good, That's What _____ _____ Is		
Nothin' Says _____ Like Somethin' from the _____		
Proud As a _____		
See the USA in Your _____		
Snap, _____, and Pop		
The Pause That _____		
We Try _____		
When It Rains It _____		
When You _____ _____ to Send the Very Best		
You Deserve a _____ Today		
You'll Wonder Where the _____ Went		
You've Come Along Way _____		

Topic VI — REMINISCENCE

SLOGANS
Leader's Guide

PURPOSE
To reminisce using famous slogans as prompts.

POSSIBLE NAMES OF SESSIONS
- *Think Back in Time!*
- *Boost Your Brain Power*
- *Commercials Worth Remembering*

BACKGROUND INFORMATION
Famous slogans have one thing in common - the company and the ad agency that created the slogan wants you to remember the company. Encouraging this fun way to reminisce may assist in restoring memories, humming jingles, and laughing.

ACTIVITY
1. Discuss how effective slogans work so that we remember them!
2. Distribute handouts and pens. Divide group into pairs and encourage participants to complete the slogan, write the advertiser, and either the year (or decade) the ad was created.
3. Reconvene. Everyone gives a rousing round of applause to the team(s) that guessed the most slogans and advertisers, and came closest to the years or decades of when they were created.

VARIATIONS
Develop a list of favorite slogans that were not mentioned in the handout, for future groups.

KEY

Slogan	Company	Year
A Little **Dab'll** Do You	Brylcreem	1950
All the **News** That's Fit to Print	New York Times	1897
Betcha Can't Eat Just **One**	Lays Chips	1963
Better Things for Better Living, Through **Chemistry**	Dupont	1935
Breakfast of **Champions**	Wheaties	1933
Don't Leave Home **Without** It	American Express	1975
Finger **Lickin'** Good	Kentucky Fried Chicken	1961
Fly the Friendly **Skies**	United Airlines	1897
Good to the Last **Drop**	Maxwell House	1926
How Do You Spell **Relief**	Rolaids	1976
I Can't Believe I **Ate** the **Whole** Thing	Alka Seltzer	1972
I'd Like to Teach the World to **Sing**	Coke	1971
I'd Walk a **Mile** for a **Camel**	Camel Cigarettes	1921
In the Valley of the **Jolly Green Giant**	Green Giant	1960
It Takes a Licking and Keeps on **Ticking**	Timex	1956
Ivory Soap – It **Floats**	Proctor & Gamble	1891
Leave the **Driving** to Us	Greyhound	1956
Like a Good Neighbor, **State Farm** Is There	State Farm Insurance	1971
Look Ma, No **Cavities**	Crest	1965
Melts in Your **Mouth** ... Not in Your **Hands**	M & M's	1956
Mmmm Good, That's What **Campbell's Soup** Is	Campbell's Soup	1931
Nothin' Says **Lovin'** Like Somethin' from the **Oven**	Poppin Fresh Pillsbury	1965
Proud As a **Peacock**	NBC	1979
See the USA in Your **Chevrolet**	Chevrolet	1957
Snap, **Crackle,** and Pop	Rice Krispies	1932
The Pause That **Refreshes**	Coca Cola	1929
We Try **Harder**	Avis	1962
When It Rains It **Pours**	Morton Salt	1914
When You **Care Enough** to Send the Very Best	Hallmark	1944
You Deserve a **Break** Today	McDonald's	1970
You'll Wonder Where the **Yellow** Went	Pepsodent	1948
You've Come Along Way **Baby**	Virginia Slims	1968

Topic VI — REMINISCENCE

Historic Dates

What do you remember about these historic dates?

A. The first person who landed on the moon was _____
- What was the year or decade? _____
- What was the name of the spacecraft? _____
- Where were you at the time and who were you with (if anyone)? _____
  _____

B. In 1963, John F. Kennedy was shot. What was the date? _____
- In what city? _____
- Who killed this president? _____
- What were you doing when you heard this news? _____
  _____

C. 9-11 is a date we remember as a tragic event when planes hit the Twin Towers in what city?
_____
- What was the year? _____
- How did you find out about it? _____
- What did you feel when you heard about it? _____

Now, let's try other, more personal, positive historic dates.

Choose one of the following and describe in detail below and on the back of the page if extra space is needed.
- The day you were married.
- The day a child of yours was born or adopted.
- The day you graduated from high school or college.
- The day you learned the truth about sex.

_____
_____
_____
_____
_____
_____

OPTIMAL WELL-BEING FOR SENIOR ADULTS I

Historic Dates
Leader's Guide

PURPOSE
To reminisce about historic dates we have as a community and those that we have personally.

POSSIBLE NAMES OF SESSIONS
- *Remember When?*
- *Reminiscing*
- *Dates of Our Lives*

BACKGROUND INFORMATION
Reminiscing in a group setting can be a powerful tool to reflect on events in our lives, with the addition of gaining perspective that time offers. When recalling important dates, it is amazing to discover the details we can remember … the surroundings, people we were with, how we felt, perhaps even the smells. Sharing these details is enriching, not only to our memories, but to our emotional state.

ACTIVITY
1. Distribute the handouts and pens.
2. Encourage group members to complete the handout.
3. Help participants fill in the blanks they may have missed.
    A. Neil Armstrong – 1969 – Apollo
    B. November 22, Dallas, Lee Harvey Oswald
    C. New York City - 2001
4. Ask group members to share what they recall from the first three events and then to share one of their own positive historic dates.

VARIATIONS
Divide group into pairs after discussing the first three events. Ask each group member to share the details of one of his/her positive historic dates. The listeners will then present as much as they recall about the details of their partners' historic dates.

NOTES
_____
_____
_____
_____
_____
_____
_____
_____
_____
_____
_____
_____
_____
_____
_____
_____
_____

Topic VII

SELF-AWARENESS
Table of Contents and Corresponding Goals for Each Section

Knowing others is intelligence; knowing yourself is true wisdom.
Mastering others is strength; mastering yourself is true power.
~ Tao Te Ching

Celebrate You! 83
To focus on one's special attributes.
To appreciate one's own uniqueness.

Give Yourself A Pat On The Back 85
To improve self-awareness and self-esteem by acknowledging one's strengths and achievements.

How I Grew To Be Who I Am 87
To do a life review activity with the universal metaphor of a tree to enhance self-awareness and self-esteem.

SEEING MY STRENGTHS 89
To increase self-awareness by recognizing one's strengths as an important part of self-advocacy.

How Does Your Garden Grow? 91
To focus on positive thoughts and the work it takes to maintain a positive outlook.

LEVEL OF UNDERSTANDING

Basic Level | Intermediate Level | High Level

Topic VII — SELF-AWARENESS

Celebrate You!

Many of us are more comfortable discussing our faults than we are at affirming our strengths.

If you want to feel good about yourself and who you are, it's important to give yourself permission to brag a little – to celebrate a unique, loving person - YOU!

Complete each sentence below with the first response that comes to your mind.

One of the ways that I am learning and growing is ...

One of the positive changes I've made recently is ...

One of the positive things I like about my body is ...

One of the positive things I like about my mind is ...

One of the positive things I like about my spirit is ...

OPTIMAL WELL-BEING FOR SENIOR ADULTS I

Celebrate You!
Leader's Guide

PURPOSE
To focus on one's special attributes.

To appreciate one's own uniqueness.

POSSIBLE NAMES OF SESSIONS
- *Strength Building*
- *Time to BRAG!*
- *Why Not Tell It Like It Is?*

BACKGROUND INFORMATION
Many of us are very self-critical; we have an easier time talking about our faults, limitations, and deficits than talking about our strengths, talents, and qualities. This exercise is designed to give participants permission and encouragement to recognize and celebrate their positive attributes.

ACTIVITY
1. Tell group members that you are giving them permission and encouragement to brag!
2. Distribute handouts and pens.
3. Ask group members to complete the sentences with examples of ways they are growing and changing, and things they like about their bodies, minds, and spirits.
4. Ask participants to share at least one of their statements with the rest of the group. If the group is large, you may wish to divide the group into smaller groups. Four is an ideal number. No one should be pressured to share a response.
5. When participants share their responses, ask them to stand up and read the statement in a convincing way – to "say it like you mean it."
6. Suggest that participants put these statements in a place where they will see them and read them on a daily basis. The boxes can even be cut apart and put in a variety of places – taped to a bathroom mirror, the side of the computer, the dashboard of the car, or inside a calendar/daily planner.

VARIATIONS
1) Discuss how media has a role in how we see ourselves. Bring examples of over-idealized men and women in pictures, headlines and captions via video clips, commercials, catalogue ads, cover of magazines, websites, etc. Discuss the consequences of those repeated images on self-control.
2) After giving group members a few minutes to write responses, ask them to share their answers to the first statement by going around the group and having each person read his or her response aloud. Allow individuals to 'pass' if they choose, but the outcome of a pass is that you must listen to compliments from other group members. For example, if a person does not share what she likes about her own spirit, the other group members will tell her something positive they appreciate about her spirit.
3) Discuss how the media portrays senior citizens, often subtly, and the stereotypes often seen.
4) Discuss well-known senior citizens who remain vibrant in the arts, politics, humanitarian, and other endeavors.

NOTES
_____
_____
_____

Topic VII — SELF-AWARENESS

Give Yourself A Pat On The Back

Doing for ourselves takes effort!
Recognizing and acknowledging what we are doing for ourselves also takes effort!
What have you done for yourself lately?

Good for Me!

being good to myself physically by _____
_____

being good to myself emotionally by _____
_____

saying _____
_____

achieving the goal of _____
_____

being patient when _____
_____

taking the time to _____
_____

keeping _____
_____

remembering _____
_____

learning _____
_____

respecting _____
_____

allowing _____
_____

OPTIMAL WELL-BEING FOR SENIOR ADULTS I

Give Yourself A Pat On The Back
Leader's Guide

PURPOSE

To improve self-awareness and self-esteem by acknowledging one's strengths and achievements.

POSSIBLE NAMES OF SESSIONS
- *Upping My Self-Talk*
- *YAY ME!*
- *Tooting My Own Horn*

BACKGROUND INFORMATION

People oftentimes develop a habit of self-critical thinking and seeing only negatives or limitations, deficits, weaknesses or problems. The results of this lead to isolation and depression. This exercise forces one to identify strengths and engage in self-appreciation.

ACTIVITY

1. Distribute handouts and pens.
2. Review as a group. Then give group members time to complete the handout individually.
3. Ask group members to find at least one statement they are comfortable reading aloud.
4. Discuss comfort levels or discomfort levels that group members have in identifying positives about themselves.
5. Challenge group members to discuss benefits and obstacles of recognizing and acknowledging positive actions taken in our lives.

VARIATIONS

1) Write on the board "Good for me…" Cut each open-ended statement into strips. Put in basket and have group members draw strips of paper and complete verbally. Encourage group members to give feedback to individuals making statements, possibly through applause or affirming statements such as "That must have been tough" or "That's worth remembering."
2) Pursue discussion of the difficulty of this exercise for youngsters vs. seniors. Are there any special challenges facing seniors when doing this type of exercise?

NOTES

_____
_____
_____
_____
_____
_____
_____
_____
_____
_____
_____

Topic VII — SELF-AWARENESS

How I Grew To Be Who I Am

1. Fruits of my labor (the later years)

I am proud of my ability to _____

_____

I am proud that I have created or helped to create _____

_____

I am proud that I stand for_____

_____

Today, I am known for _____

_____

2. My growth and development (the middle years)

I overcame_____

_____

I learned_____

_____

Back then I was known as_____

_____

3. My roots (the early years)

My cultural heritage and background is _____

_____

The people who raised me are/were _____

_____

Values I was taught as a youngster were _____

_____

OPTIMAL WELL-BEING FOR SENIOR ADULTS I

How I Grew To Be Who I Am
Leader's Guide

PURPOSE
To do a life review activity with the universal metaphor of a tree to enhance self-awareness and self-esteem.

POSSIBLE NAMES OF SESSIONS
- *My Life in a Nutshell … or Tree*
- *Where Did I Come From? Where Am I Now?*
- *My Tree of Life*

BACKGROUND INFORMATION
The theme of using a tree in artwork and therapy is well explored, and its universal nature remains appealing. This simple activity explores people's beginnings, their development, and who they are today. Life reviews can enhance self-awareness and self-esteem, and be life affirming.

ACTIVITY
1. Prepare a flipchart or dry erase board with a similar tree as the one on the handout. Write "LIFE IS LIKE A TREE."
2. Ask the group members what the roots might symbolize and write all responses at the bottom of the tree. Accept all answers. Then ask what the bark might symbolize and write all responses. Lastly, ask group members what the top branches or fruit might symbolize and write all responses.
3. Distribute handouts and pens.
4. Discuss group responses and compare with concepts on the handout.
5. Give group members ten to fifteen minutes to complete the handout starting with #1 and finishing with #3.
6. Divide group into pairs for five to ten minutes to share responses.
7. Reconvene and ask group members what the most interesting insight they gained from doing this exercise.

VARIATIONS
1) What was missing from the handout? Develop additional questions for each section and discuss.
2) Suggest that group members share this work with those who are interested (e.g., volunteers, family members, neighbors, friends).

NOTES
_____
_____
_____
_____
_____
_____
_____
_____
_____
_____
_____
_____

Topic VII — SELF-AWARENESS

SEEING MY STRENGTHS
That's Who I Am

Focusing on only problems, illnesses, disabilities and losses is an easy trap to fall into. Instead, what might happen if we look at what we have going for us?

In the following categories, write at least one of your strengths.

Skills

Relationships

Emotional or Physical Health

Activities & Interests

Knowledge

Life Experience(s)

Other Strengths

OPTIMAL WELL-BEING FOR SENIOR ADULTS I

SEEING MY STRENGTHS
Leader's Guide

PURPOSE
To increase self-awareness by recognizing one's strengths as an important part of self-advocacy.

POSSIBLE NAMES OF SESSIONS
- *Strengths R US*
- *My Assets*
- *Using My Strengths for Good*

BACKGROUND INFORMATION
The healthcare system documents and gets reimbursed for looking at deficits and problems. Unfortunately, people are often viewed that way as well. By looking at strengths, we encourage the senior adults to see themselves as abled rather that dis-abled, resourceful, and able to make good choices. As healthcare professionals we can refer to these strengths in conversations with the senior, with family members and friends, and with professional staff. We can also note these in documentation.

ACTIVITY
1. Distribute handouts and pens.
2. Explain the basic concept of recognizing that everyone's path has obstacles. Our strengths help us to overcome those obstacles.
3. Allow group members ten minutes to complete the handout. Clarify as needed.
4. Divide group into triads and give them ten to fifteen minutes to share.
5. Reconvene and ask group members to share what was learned.
6. Ask:
    a. How can knowing your strengths be helpful to you? To your healthcare team? To those people who are close to you?
    b. Why is talking about strengths difficult for some people?
    c. How did it feel to talk about what would happen to you if you focused on strengths rather than deficits, inabilities, and losses?

VARIATIONS
Ask group members to share this handout with a person with whom they have a close relationship, and to ask for feedback.

NOTES
___
___
___
___
___
___
___
___
___
___
___
___
___

How Does Your Garden Grow?

NEGATIVE

Most Powerful Negative Thoughts

POSITIVE

Most Powerful Positive Thoughts

OPTIMAL WELL-BEING FOR SENIOR ADULTS I

How Does Your Garden Grow?
Leader's Guide

PURPOSE
To focus on positive thoughts and the work it takes to maintain a positive outlook.

POSSIBLE NAMES OF SESSIONS
- *Tending the Garden*
- *Positivity Is My Goal!*
- *Flower Power*

BACKGROUND INFORMATION
Negative thoughts are powerful and pervasive, and they can "choke out" positive thoughts. Writing persistent negative thoughts increases awareness of them, and can lead to more rapid thought-stopping. This in turn can lead to the ability to change negative thoughts into positive thoughts.

ACTIVITY
1. Introduce topic by reviewing background information.
2. Distribute handouts and pens.
3. Ask group members to think about their negative thoughts. Acknowledge that these might be a carryover from childhood. Ask them to write these thoughts in the left "weeds" box. Offer examples: *"No one cares about me." "I'm not good enough." "I'm too old for that." "I'm not smart enough."*
4. Ask group members to think of positive thoughts they routinely say to themselves. Ask them to write these thoughts in the right "plants" box. Offer examples: *"I have friends and family who can help me." "I've managed tougher things than this before." "I have faith." "I can do this!"*
5. Ask the group members to identify the most prominent negative thoughts and positive thoughts at the bottom of each box, and share.
6. Process by formulating individual plans to maintain positive thoughts, or having a "weed-free garden." These plans might include spending more time or less time with certain people, activities, and involvements, or putting a penny in a "charity jar" every time a negative thought recurs.

VARIATIONS
1) Give group members small plants as a symbolic, token gift upon completion of session or program.
2) Discuss the consequences that negative thinking has on one's healthy well-being, positive self-esteem, fruitful relationships, and daily energy level. Demonstrate this through skits generated by group members.

NOTES
_____
_____
_____
_____
_____
_____
_____
_____

Topic VIII
SOCIAL SKILLS
Table of Contents and Corresponding Goals for Each Section

When people become lonely and isolated, whatever social skills they have tend to atrophy from misuse.
~ Chris Segrin

Celebrating the Seasons 95
To increase awareness of common and special interests during different times of the year.

A Dozen Effective Communication Tips 97
To increase awareness of twelve effective communication strategies.

Acts of Loving Kindness 99
To recognize how acts of loving kindness to others add to one's quality of life.

Seniors Speak Out 101
To increase functional self-expression in the area of social skills.

What I Like To Do 103
To increase leisure and social interest.

LEVEL OF UNDERSTANDING
Basic Level | Intermediate Level | High Level

Topic VIII — SOCIAL SKILLS

Celebrating the Seasons

Describe activities that you can enjoy throughout the year.

Summer
1. _____
2. _____
3. _____

Winter
1. _____
2. _____
3. _____

Spring
1. _____
2. _____
3. _____

Fall
1. _____
2. _____
3. _____

HOLIDAYS
1. _____
2. _____
3. _____

Celebrating the Seasons
Leader's Guide

PURPOSE
To increase awareness of common and special interests during different times of the year.

POSSIBLE NAMES OF SESSIONS
- *Enjoy the Season*
- *Special Times of Year*
- *Four Seasons*

BACKGROUND INFORMATION
Seasons present different activities and celebrations. Whether preparing for them or engaging in them, they give structure and continuity to our lives. People may prefer certain times of the year to other times, depending on their experiences and the activities available during those seasons and holidays. This activity allows group members to learn more about their common interests and develop awareness and trust. This handout can be used for any time during the year, with emphasis on events around that time as well as throughout the year.

ACTIVITY
1. Distribute handouts and pens.
2. Ask group members to write three events, focusing on what they enjoy, people they are with, and where they go.
3. Discuss the following questions:
   a. Who introduced these events and traditions into your life?
   b. Which did you develop on your own?
   c. Which bring the most meaning to you today?
   d. Are special foods, flowers, or people associated with these celebrations?
4. Discuss ways that seasons and celebrations are experienced differently at different stages of life.
5. Discuss ways to adapt celebrations considering the realities of the present situation.

VARIATIONS
1) Use this handout in conjunction with *Talk About Feelings, page 35*.
2) Ask group members to identify these emotions, which they associate with each season.

NOTES
_____
_____
_____
_____
_____
_____
_____
_____
_____
_____
_____

A Dozen Effective Communication Tips

Fill in the blanks using the word key below.

1. Listen more and _____ _____.
2. Ask after you briefly _____, "Did I get that right?"
3. Confess if you weren't _____, say that, and ask the person to _____ it.
4. Use fewer words and get to the point _____.
5. You do not need to _____ _____; listening is all that most people need.
6. Use "_____ _____ _____" statements VS "You made me feel..."
7. Be aware of _____ language and avoid or retract if possible.
8. Find _____ environments for important conversations.
9. Create a time when _____ communication can take place VS saying something important when the listener is "not quite there."
10. Be the listener to want to have when _____ _____ _____; avoid interrupting.
11. Focus on the speaker's _____, not about what you are about to say.
12. Watch and be aware of _____ about what you are hearing. Then you can decide if you want to share rather than blurting out something that may be harmful or hurtful, and that you may regret later.

Word Key

blaming	paraphrase
distraction-free	quickly
effective	repeat
fix it	talk less
I feel when	words
judgments	you are speaking
listening	

OPTIMAL WELL-BEING FOR SENIOR ADULTS I

A Dozen Effective Communication Tips
Leader's Guide

PURPOSE
To increase awareness of twelve effective communication strategies.

POSSIBLE NAMES OF SESSIONS
- *Let's Be Clear*
- *Listen Up.*
- *Effective Communications Strategies*

BACKGROUND INFORMATION
All too often we fall into ruts pertaining to our communications, e.g., interrupting too much, thinking about what we are going to say rather than listening, daydreaming when listening, etc. This handout provides an opportunity to challenge current communication styles, and clearly introduce and guide us to more effective communication.

ACTIVITY
1. Introduce concepts from Background Information,
2. Distribute handouts and pencils.
3. As a group:
   a. Ask a group member to read number one aloud. Then, as a group, try to find the correct answer in the answer key below.

Word Key	
blaming	paraphrase
distraction-free	quickly
effective	repeat
fix it	talk less
I feel when	words
judgments	you are speaking
listening	

   b. Instruct group members to write it in the blank on their handout.
   c. Ask group members to honestly assess how they rate at each skill (1 being the lowest and 10 being the highest) and write it next to the number.
   d. Continue with all twelve tips.
4. Ask group members to identify one or two of the self-rated lower numbers on the handouts that would be worthy of focusing on to improve communication. Discuss as a group and encourage support for taking this important step.

VARIATIONS
1) Create role plays using group members' examples to illustrate each strategy, or prepare index cards with role plays prior to group.
2) Discuss each tip using different relationships in mind to explore communication traps.
   Examples: doctor / patient - child / parent - friend / friend.

NOTES
_____
_____
_____
_____
_____
_____

Acts of Loving Kindness

We all have choices.
We can choose to feel sorry for ourselves, we can be angry about life's shortcomings,
and we can be irritable and resentful. We can also choose to be giving and loving.
Performing acts of loving kindness is an approach towards healthful living.
It is possible to be loving and giving despite obstacles we face.

By giving of ourselves, we might also gain.
What might you gain if you choose to perform acts of loving kindness?

Here are some ideas to begin. Fill in the blanks.

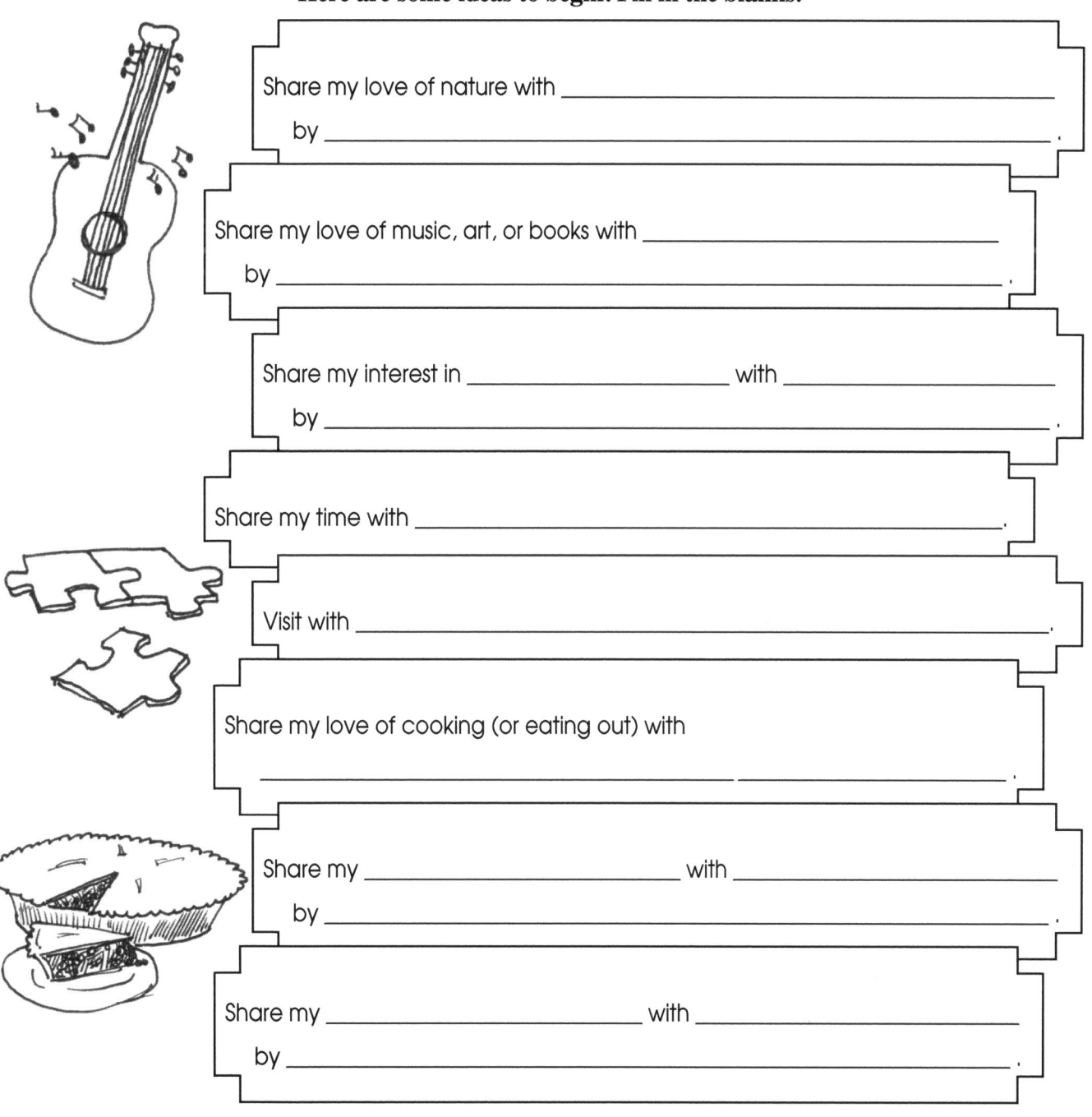

Share my love of nature with _____
   by _____.

Share my love of music, art, or books with _____
   by _____.

Share my interest in _____ with _____
   by _____.

Share my time with _____.

Visit with _____.

Share my love of cooking (or eating out) with
_____.

Share my _____ with _____
   by _____.

Share my _____ with _____
   by _____.

Acts of Loving Kindness
Leader's Guide

PURPOSE
To recognize how acts of loving kindness to others add to the quality of life.

POSSIBLE NAMES OF SESSIONS
- *Kindness Counts!*
- *No Time Like the Present to Start!*
- *Random Acts of Kindness*

BACKGROUND INFORMATION
Choosing acts of loving kindness is emphasized rather than choosing anger, irritability, and resentment. It is beneficial to look at semi-retirement, retirement, or a time of having fewer responsibilities, as a time to share. Sharing allows for a sense of connectedness with others and a desire to share a passion or enjoyment. Ideas to be shared are limitless and can be inspirational!

ACTIVITY
1. Begin with a discussion of what people remember about grandparents, older relatives or neighbors. Focus especially on how they spent their time with those people.
2. Distribute handouts with pens.
3. Explain the concept of the activity using the top paragraph on the handout and the background information.
4. Read the following examples to your clients.
   a. Share my love of nature with <u>my granddaughter</u> by <u>taking her for walks in the park.</u>
   b. Share my love of music, art, or books with <u>my friend</u> by <u>going to museum events.</u>
5. Give group members ten minutes to complete handouts.
6. Encourage creativity and unique responses.
7. Share responses and problem-solve ways that these ideas could actually happen.
8. Discuss obstacles to action, and supports to facilitate action.

VARIATIONS
1) Create exciting groups, programs, or booklets with participants by sharing any of the ideas that group members were enthusiastic about sharing. For example: "Bake a Bread with Marsha," "Listen to Violin by Harry," "Plant Seedlings with Luke."
2) Show a video clip of a favorite commercial, movie or TV show exemplifying an act of loving kindness from a senior adult.

NOTES
_____
_____
_____
_____
_____
_____
_____
_____
_____
_____

Seniors Speak Out

Host: *Hello and welcome to our Seniors Speak Out talk show.*

   I am your host _____

   Today, our guest is _____

   Please tell the viewers a little bit about yourself.

Guest responds: _____

Host: *Compare your communication skills of today and those of five years ago.*

Guest responds: _____

Host: *Tell the group about a time in which you could have been more assertive.*

Guest responds: _____

Host: *Describe a time in the last six months when you were "very sociable."*

Guest responds: _____

Host: *How would you rate your 'being a good friend' skill? 0=poor 10=excellent?*

Guest responds: _____

Host: *Please tell the viewers about one of your best social skills.*

Guest responds: _____

Host: *How do you meet new and interesting people?*

Guest responds: _____

Host: *Now we will take a few questions from the audience.*

Guest responds: _____

OPTIMAL WELL-BEING FOR SENIOR ADULTS I

Seniors Speak Out
Leader's Guide

PURPOSE
To increase functional self-expression in the area of social skills.

POSSIBLE NAMES OF SESSIONS
- Here's …………
- HEADLINE: New Talk Show In Town
- Who's Who?

BACKGROUND INFORMATION
Many people feel threatened or intimidated to share thoughts and feelings in a group setting. They may become quiet and withdrawn. This activity facilitates speaking in a group within a highly structured and supportive setting. Social skills is a great topic! How we relate to others is very important when thinking about overall life satisfaction.

ACTIVITY
1. Briefly discuss the topic of social skills.
2. Explain to the group members that they are going to be asked to discuss this topic by attending a new talk show called *Seniors Speak Out*.
3. Distribute copies of the handout.
4. Read aloud.
5. Each group member will be designated a role, including: 1 host, 1 guest, and audience members to ask questions, depending on group size, and remaining audience.
6. Designate these roles to each group member by one of three methods:
   a. Have group members choose roles independently.
   b. Have group members choose slips of paper (roles as stated in number 5, above) out of a basket.
   c. The group leader designates specific roles to certain group members.
7. Explain the responsibilities of each talk show member as follows:
   a. Host – welcomes the audience, reads the script to the guest.
   b. Guest – responds to the hosts questions.
   c. Audience with questions – after all questions from the script are answered, these group members ask appropriate questions for the guest to answer.
   d. Remaining audience – listens to the interactions of host and guest, applauds when appropriate, and critiques the host and guest on their social skills at the end of the talk show.
8. Using the designated roles, proceed with the *Seniors Speak Out* talk show.
9. When complete, elicit helpful feedback from audience on how well the host/guest played their roles.
10. Encourage group members to switch roles and continue to proceed with the talk show until all have had a chance to be the host or guest, or as long as time permits.

VARIATIONS
1) Make or bring props to create a fun Talk Show setting: microphone, desk, cue cards saying 'applause,' etc.
2) Develop other game show scripts on topics of interest: taking time for leisure and fun, being a grandparent, managing money.

What I Like To Do

Name _____

Put an **H** for the activity you have a **HIGH** level of interest.
Put an **L** for the activity you have a **LOW** level of interest.
Put an **N** for the activity you have a **NO** level of interest.
Add any other activities in which you have an interest on the "other" lines.

ART
- appreciation of art ____
- craft projects ____
- museums ____
- other _____

COMPUTERS
- games ____
- internet/email ____
- online shopping ____
- other _____

EXERCISE
- aerobic activities ____
- competitive sports ____
- stretch activities ____
- other _____

FOOD RELATED
- bake ____
- cook ____
- eat out ____
- other _____

HISTORY
- local ____
- military ____
- world ____
- other _____

MOVIES
- action ____
- comedy ____
- drama ____
- other _____

MUSIC
- listen ____
- play instrument ____
- sing ____
- other _____

NATURE
- garden ____
- indoors looking out ____
- outdoors ____
- other _____

READ/LISTEN
- audio books ____
- books ____
- magazine/newspaper ____
- other _____

SOCIAL
- conversation ____
- games/cards ____
- parties ____
- other _____

SPORTS
- events ____
- play ____
- television ____
- other _____

TV
- action ____
- comedy ____
- drama ____
- other _____

WRITE
- journal ____
- letters/notes ____
- stories/poems ____
- other _____

OTHER
- _____
- _____
- _____
- _____

OPTIMAL WELL-BEING FOR SENIOR ADULTS I

What I Like To Do
Leader's Guide

PURPOSE
To increase leisure and social interests.

POSSIBLE NAMES OF SESSIONS
- *Time Well Spent*
- *Choices, Choices, Choices*
- *Ban Boredom*

BACKGROUND INFORMATION
Many seniors struggle with sedentary lifestyles, loneliness, and isolation. There are many reasons they may need to rethink their leisure pursuits. People may be retired with more free time then they had before. Physical challenges might limit prior leisure involvements, such as decreased eyesight, a stroke, or unsteady hands.

ACTIVITY
1. Bring several leisure interest items to the group: a romance novel, a history book, CD of music or relaxation exercises, needlepoint, kitchen mixing bowl and spoon, hammer, word search puzzle book, baseball, package of flower or vegetable seeds, deck of cards, etc.
2. As you show each item, ask group members to say if the item is of high, low, or no interest to them.
3. Compare results.
4. Explain that leisure choices are individual and sometimes change as we get older.
5. Distribute handouts and pens.
6. Allow group members ten minutes to complete the handout.
7. Discuss the results with emphasis on the need to engage in social and leisure activities to combat sedentary life styles, loneliness and isolation.
8. Develop action plans based on responses and discussion.

VARIATIONS
1) If several members have similar interests, pair or group them together to make plans and support each other.
2) Create a second session with a local older adult enthusiast about a popular leisure topic. This person can demonstrate this skill and be a great role model.

NOTES

_____
_____
_____
_____
_____
_____
_____
_____
_____
_____
_____
_____

Topic IX
STAYING ACTIVE & YOUNG AT HEART
Table of Contents and Corresponding Goals for Each Section

> *The key to successful aging is to pay as little attention to it as possible.*
> ~ Judith Regan

Finding Humor Today! 107
To recognize that humor is a powerful way to stay young at heart.

Empowering Myself To Be Active 109
To recognize the obstacles and benefits of being active as a senior, and to set action plans in motion.

Energy Conservation 111
To increase knowledge of energy conservation, promoting safety in ADL's (activities of daily living) and home management. To increase time for leisure or social pursuits due to increased energy and decreased fatigue.

I Want My Independence 113
To evaluate perceptions and actions which lend themselves to independence in seniors.

What Can I Do 115
To become educated about four strategies for good brain health.

LEVEL OF UNDERSTANDING

 Basic Level    Intermediate Level    High Level

Topic IX — STAYING ACTIVE & YOUNG AT HEART

Finding Humor Today!

Look for terms that relate to humor.
(vertical, horizontal and diagonal)

G	I	G	G	L	E	S	I	B	O	N	N	F	U	C	M	S	C
A	G	E	S	P	O	N	T	A	N	E	O	U	S	R	I	U	O
M	O	L	E	R	N	T	P	O	S	I	T	I	V	E	R	N	P
E	C	H	E	I	C	H	U	C	K	L	E	S	A	A	D	I	I
S	L	O	P	E	N	D	O	R	P	H	I	N	S	T	H	T	N
T	G	O	M	O	V	I	E	S	L	L	U	M	B	I	A	E	G
H	O	R	E	E	I	R	T	O	Y	S	A	E	H	V	E	S	S
E	H	M	I	L	D	Q	H	E	A	L	M	Y	O	E	E	C	K
R	E	N	S	N	G	Y	T	H	E	M	U	F	F	U	N	I
A	A	R	D	V	A	S	T	A	R	I	M	J	O	U	P	Y	L
P	L	I	G	H	T	M	E	R	R	Y	O	U	L	L	A	L
E	I	N	L	E	R	I	T	M	A	T	I	K	T	H	I	N	N
U	N	D	E	R	A	L	A	U	G	H	T	E	R	A	F	E	Z
T	G	O	X	E	M	E	Z	P	E	P	R	E	E	T	T	Y	A
I	N	R	I	G	A	W	O	R	T	M	E	D	I	C	I	N	E
C	O	N	T	A	G	I	O	U	S	A	G	F	U	N	N	Y	E
O	M	E	R	E	L	A	X	A	T	I	O	N	M	A	G	S	K
D	I	S	T	R	A	C	T	I	O	N	S	N	A	P	E	R	S

CHUCKLES	FUNNY	LAUGHTER	RELAXATION
COMEDY	GAMES	LIGHT	SMILE
CONTAGIOUS	GIGGLE	MEDICINE	SPONTANEOUS
COPINGSKILL	GLEE	MIRTH	THERAPEUTIC
CREATIVE	GRIN	MOVIES	TOYS
DISTRACTION	HEALING	PLAYFUL	UNITES
ENDORPHINS	JOKE	POSITIVE	UPLIFTING

© 2016 WHOLE PERSON ASSOCIATES, 101 WEST 2ND STREET, SUITE 203, DULUTH MN 55802 • 800-247-6789 • WHOLEPERSON.COM

OPTIMAL WELL-BEING FOR SENIOR ADULTS I

Finding Humor Today!
Leader's Guide

PURPOSE
To recognize that humor is a powerful way to stay young at heart.

POSSIBLE NAMES OF SESSIONS
- *The Search for Humor*
- *Laughter Keeps You Young*
- *Laughter is Good Medicine*

BACKGROUND INFORMATION
Humor is a universal language and is good for the body and the soul. Finding humor is an active process that lightens the mood, brings people together, and has a tremendous healing effect.

ACTIVITY
1. Write the Key Words at the bottom of the handout on the dry erase board.
2. Discuss what each term means and how it relates to humor.
3. Distribute handouts and pens. Allow group members ten minutes to find as many of the twenty-eight terms as possible.
4. Applaud the winner(s) with the most circled answers.

VARIATIONS
Give handouts in the evening group for "homework" and then show a comedy movie to integrate knowledge with the activity.

ANSWER KEY

NOTES
_____
_____
_____
_____
_____

Topic IX — STAYING ACTIVE & YOUNG AT HEART

Empowering Myself To Be Active

Staying active and safe as a senior adult can be very challenging. Peers may become less active, it may be difficult to push yourself out the door, and it may seem fruitless.
BUT, the consequences of being inactive may be damaging.
Write in your own comments on the blank lines.

IF I don't stay active, I will …

- feel tightness of joints and muscles. _____
- have less energy. _____
- feel and look out of shape. _____
- worry about my physical condition. _____
- feel bored. _____
- be less interesting to be around. _____
- not make healthy food choices _____

The rewards of staying active might be a quality-of-life-saver!
Here are a few helpful tips that might get you up and moving.

Fill in the blanks with honest and realistic responses

- **Do not overlook the simple things in life** – walking and/or gardening.
  Both of these activities can have great benefits! Which one are you most likely to do?
  ☐ Walking   ☐ Gardening
- **Other than walking and gardening activities, pick an activity you like.** If you don't like competitive sports, don't choose one! A hint to activity success is choosing what you like!
- **What activity do you enjoy that you can do, even if it needs to be modified?**

  _____
- **Do you like doing activities alone or with someone?**
  ☐ Alone   ☐ With Someone
- **If alone, what's an activity you can do alone?**

  _____
- **If with someone, who is someone you can contact who will participate with you?**

  _____

ACTION PLAN: What safety measures are needed?
(Example: Use walker, comfortable shoes, do not walk alone on icy sidewalks, etc.)

OPTIMAL WELL-BEING FOR SENIOR ADULTS I

Empowering Myself To Be Active
Leader's Guide

PURPOSE
To recognize the obstacles and benefits of being active as a senior, and to set action plans in motion.

POSSIBLE NAMES OF SESSIONS
- *Let's GO!*
- *Active Lifestyle*
- *Do It Now!*

BACKGROUND INFORMATION
For many people the notion of exercise conjures up sweaty gyms, fanatics, athletes, hard work, and sore muscles. A preferred way to look at it might be "being active." This more inclusive term might be appealing and less threatening and may generate activities that can easily be included in an active and safe lifestyle.

ACTIVITY
1. Describe typical consequences when people don't lead an active lifestyle. List on the board. This list may include the following:
   - Tired
   - No energy
   - Irritable
   - Never leave the house
   - Feel every ache and pain
2. Lead the group in a leisurely five-minute walk (outside if possible).
3. Return and discuss how people feel. Hopefully responses will include the following: *more energy, more alive, etc.*
4. Distribute handouts and pens.
5. Allow group members ten minutes to complete entire handout except 'Action Plan.'
6. Discuss possible obstacles to being active as a senior. Responses may include the following:
   - Fear of breaking a bone
   - Lack of financial resources
   - Not wanting to take a walk alone
   - Bad weather
   - Too many things to do at home
7. Support group members in addressing these issues safely and realistically, and encourage group problem solving if appropriate.
8. Help group members design Action Plans at the bottom of the page. Explain that the aim is to be committed to an idea and to gain forward motion.
9. Share as a group.

VARIATIONS
1) Depending on the group members' interests and action plans, make realistic plans. Examples:
   - A once a week table tennis tournament
   - A morning walking group
   - A monthly bowling group
2) Bring possible motivators or conveniences to session and share. *Example: Padded socks, power bars, music, light weights, etc.*

NOTES
_____
_____
_____
_____

Topic IX — STAYING ACTIVE & YOUNG AT HEART

Energy Conservation
means saving your energy for what you need it for most!

You might be coming home after some type of illness, procedure, or episode that has been especially difficult or tiring. It might take your body and mind a while to recover. You don't want to expend your energy on things that don't really matter, and then find that you do not have energy for what really matters.

Some Energy Conservation Helpful Hints

GENERAL HINTS	SPECIFIC HINTS
Always • Sit rather than stand. • Have objects (tools, equipment, utensils) close by and easy to reach. • Take more breaks rather than fewer breaks. • Use adaptive equipment if it is safer and easier. • Be willing to ask for help if you need it. • Consider accepting offers for help. • Relax the 'perfectionist' attitude. • _____ • _____ • _____ • _____ • _____ • _____	**Cooking** • Use one-dish oven meals such as casseroles or crock pots. • Plan meals ahead to ensure having all of the needed ingredients. • _____ • _____ **Shopping** • Check on grocery delivery services in your area and use if possible. • Have someone accompany you to the store to assist with the lifting and the carrying. • _____ • _____ **Bathing** • Sponge bathing can be an alternative to showers or tub baths. • Organize yourself with all the things you need before you begin. • _____ • _____

OPTIMAL WELL-BEING FOR SENIOR ADULTS I

Energy Conservation
Leader's Guide

PURPOSE
To increase knowledge of energy conservation, promoting safety in ADL's (activities in daily living) and home management. To increase time for leisure or social pursuits due to increased energy and decreased fatigue.

POSSIBLE NAMES OF SESSIONS
- *Conserve Your Energy*
- *Perfectionism Just Won't Work Now!*
- *I'll Save My Energy For* _____

BACKGROUND INFORMATION
This activity works well with those who are coming home after a hospitalization. Energy conservation relates to healing; it takes energy to heal and to recover. Obstacles to energy conservation may include a perfectionist attitude, lack of supports, and being unaware of energy conservation techniques.

ACTIVITY
1. Introduce activity with Background Information.
2. Distribute handouts and pens.
3. Review the left portion of the handout with the group members. Use each bullet point as a possibility for a discussion. Develop educational opportunities at any point, e.g., bring adaptive equipment to group and demonstrate (kitchen timer, raised toilet seat, wheeled cart, long-handled grabber, etc.).
   Ask group members to make applicable notes on the blank lines.
4. Continue by discussing the right portion of the handout using the blank lines to share additional thoughts or ideas from the group.
5. After the handout is completed, make a list on the board of things people will do with their conserved energy (play with grandchildren, watch television, read, go out to eat, pursue a hobby or interest, play games on the computer, etc.).

VARIATIONS
1) Use role plays as a way to practice offering and accepting help.
2) Develop index cards of situations that are potentially energy intensive (cleaning house, traveling, lawn work and gardening, getting ready for birthdays and holidays, doing laundry, dressing, buying gifts, or any others that you feel group members might face.) Have group members choose a card. Ask them to think of three possible ways to conserve energy with each situation.

NOTES
_____
_____
_____
_____
_____
_____
_____
_____
_____
_____

Topic IX — STAYING ACTIVE & YOUNG AT HEART

I Want My Independence

**Independence means different things to different people.
For some folks it means living completely by themselves,
for others it means living with others and accepting help in certain areas,
but doing things as independently as possible in other areas.
And yet, for others, it's somewhere in the middle.**

Most of us like to feel as if we are in control (or at least partial control!) and struggle with the balance between keeping ourselves as independent as possible and allowing others to help us.

Fear of becoming dependent can be overwhelming and creates anxiety. As with most issues, it's better to talk about fears rather than let them stay inside buried or hidden.

Below are some thought-provoking questions to address these concerns.

The challenges I face in aging are (financial, physical, emotional, etc.) _____

_____

_____

I feel that asking for help means I'm a failure.   Circle: TRUE   or   FALSE

I feel that accepting help means I'm a failure.   Circle: TRUE   or   FALSE

I am pleasant to be around when I do need help.   Circle: TRUE   or   FALSE

Read this checklist and honestly assess if you are helping yourself to be as independent as possible. Check what you do on a regular basis.

- ☐ I give myself extra time, so I don't need to rush.
- ☐ I use adaptive equipment or aids that were recommended.
- ☐ I wear my glasses and/or hearing aid as needed.
- ☐ I walk with my walker or cane as recommended by my therapist or doctor.
- ☐ I take my medications as prescribed.
- ☐ I avoid clutter, throw rugs, or anything that could create an unsafe atmosphere.
- ☐ I spend money on things or services I need to help me be as independent as possible.
- ☐ I arrange my home or living area in a way that is safe, handy, and easy-to-manage.
- ☐ I recognize that stairways and bathtubs are danger zones, and I'm careful to take special precautions in those places.
- ☐ I accept help when needed.

I Want My Independence
Leader's Guide

PURPOSE
To evaluate perceptions and actions which lend themselves to independence in seniors.

POSSIBLE NAMES OF SESSIONS
- *I Want It MY Way*
- *As Independent … As Possible*
- *Realistic Aging*

BACKGROUND INFORMATION
A majority of seniors face the fear of losing control and their independence. It might be a healthy approach to discuss fears in an open, nonjudgmental, and realistic atmosphere. Recognizing personal fears and attitudes, and making personal choices about the environment, adaptive aids and services may encourage independence.

ACTIVITY
1. Write the word INDEPENDENCE in large letters on the board for everyone to see.
2. Ask group members what words or images come to mind when they see that word. List responses for everyone to see.
3. Explain that most people want to be as independent as possible and that there are attitudes and actions that might promote that.
4. Distribute handouts and pens.
5. First, focus on the thought-provoking statements towards the top of the handout and allow members to share responses.
6. Proceed to the remaining statements below and encourage sharing of actions that people do or don't do in order to maintain independence.
7. Ask each person to have one action plan, some action to take which might promote independence. This might include discussing an attitude with a loved one, buying a piece of adaptive equipment, rearranging a shelf, or pulling up a floor rug.

VARIATIONS
1) Bring a few adaptive equipment catalogues for people to peruse.
2) Find a poem, quote or saying, about the value of independence and the value of accepting help as well.

NOTES
_____
_____
_____
_____
_____
_____
_____
_____
_____
_____
_____
_____

Topic IX — STAYING ACTIVE & YOUNG AT HEART

What Can I Do

Q: What can I do to support good brain health?
A: Engage in a healthy life style!

1. Stay Active

- Exercise
- Enjoy a healthy life style
- _____
- _____
- _____
- _____
- _____
- _____
- _____
- _____
- _____
- _____

2. Keep Learning

- Explore unfamiliar ground
- Take a class
- _____
- _____
- _____
- _____
- _____
- _____
- _____
- _____
- _____
- _____

3. Connect

- Create a strong social network
- Feel that what you do makes a difference
- _____
- _____
- _____
- _____
- _____
- _____
- _____
- _____
- _____
- _____

4. Protect Arteries

- Keep blood pressure and weight at healthy levels
- Eat healthy
- _____
- _____
- _____
- _____
- _____
- _____
- _____
- _____
- _____
- _____

OPTIMAL WELL-BEING FOR SENIOR ADULTS I

What Can I Do
Leader's Guide

PURPOSE

To become educated about four strategies for good brain health.

POSSIBLE NAMES OF SESSIONS

- *How To Keep My Brain Working*
- *Use It or Lose It*
- *Brain-Healthy Activities*

BACKGROUND INFORMATION

While it is true that processing speed slows as we age, memory decline is NOT inevitable with age. Staying active and engaging in good brain health affects every role of a senior. (Example: family member, caregiver, volunteer, friend, healthy nutritionist, reader, game player, etc.)

ACTIVITY

1. Divide group into four subgroups, assigning each a number: 1, 2, 3 or 4.
2. Distribute handouts and pens. Review the question and answer at the top of the page.
3. Dispel any myths about aging and loss of brain function with focus on four strategies stating what we can do for good brain health.
4. Assign each subgroup a corresponding strategy to discuss. Write specific, realistic examples in that category. Allow ten minutes for this activity.
   Example: **1. Stay Active**
      Exercise: *walk, tennis, hike, swim, yoga, tai chi, golf, weight lift, bike*
      Enjoy an Active Lifestyle: *take stairs vs. elevator; garden and clean house vs. get assistance; walk to mailbox; make food from scratch vs. from a box or jar.*
5. Reconvene and instruct subgroups to present their ideas to the entire group. Encourage note-taking on handouts.

VARIATIONS

Facilitate an activity from each of the four ideas presented.
   Example: Walk 5 minutes; teach a few historical facts; play a game.

NOTES

_____
_____
_____
_____
_____
_____
_____
_____
_____
_____
_____
_____

Topic X

THINKING SKILLS
Table of Contents and Corresponding Goals for Each Section

If you think you can, you can. And if you think you can't, you're right.
~ Mary Kay Ash

The "And" Game 119
To engage thinking skills with brain-boosting activities.

The "And" Game - Challenge Edition 121
To engage thinking skills with challenging brain-boosting activities.

CURRENT EVENTS! 123
To engage cognitively about what is happening in the world with possible benefits of reality orientation, drawing attention away from an internal focus and moving towards an external focus, and developing interesting conversation and social interaction on relevant topics.

Which / Witch is It? 125
To stimulate thinking by using homophones as a brain-boosting prompt.

Mental Toughness – The Thinker Quiz 127
To increase thought-processing and group involvement by answering questions, listening, and sharing.

LEVEL OF UNDERSTANDING

 Basic Level    Intermediate Level    High Level

The "And" Game

& & & & & & & & & & & & & & &

Try These Brain Boosters for fun!

Fill in the blanks with the best possible answer.

Abercrombie and _____

Amos and _____

Bagels and _____

Batman and _____

Beauty and the _____

Bert and _____

Bonnie and _____

Cheese and _____

Cops and _____

Dagwood and _____

Earth, Wind and _____

Fibber McGee and _____

Fred and _____

George and _____

Harpo, Groucho, Zeppo, and _____

Hot and _____

In and _____

Jack and _____

Kiss and _____

Liver and _____

Lone Ranger and _____

Macaroni and _____

Peanut butter and _____

Peter and the _____

Peter, Paul, and _____

Porgy and _____

Pots and _____

Reading, writing, and _____

Red, white and _____

Salt and _____

Sears and _____

Sodom and _____

Spencer Tracy and _____

The birds and the _____

The Good, the Bad, and the _____

Up, up and _____

War and _____

Washer and _____

The "And" Game
Leader's Guide

PURPOSE
To engage thinking skills with brain-boosting activity.

POSSIBLE NAMES OF SESSIONS
- *Think Again!*
- *AND So On!*
- *Come On … You Can Do It!*

BACKGROUND INFORMATION
Cognitive activities can be success-oriented, stimulating, and fun. The prompts that come before the "and" are from a variety of sources including TV, books, songs, poems, food, childhood games, and idioms.

ACTIVITY
1. Introduce the concept of using the brain like a muscle. The brain needs exercising, and the way to do it is by challenging it.
2. Distribute handouts and pens. Instruct group members to write the best answers on the lines. Even though there are many answers that might be right, there is one preferred answer.
3. Allow group members as much time as it takes to complete the handout.
4. Use the key at the bottom of the page to check for answers.
5. Share responses.
6. Process the value of challenging the mind in fun and enjoyable ways.

VARIATIONS
1) Use as a timed activity, giving the winner a round of applause.
2) Play in pairs with one person giving the clues and one answering.
3) Allow one hint if the guesser doesn't get it right on the first try.

ANSWER KEY

Abercrombie and **Fitch**
Amos and **Andy**
Bagels and **lox**
Batman and **Robin**
Beauty and the **Beast**
Bert and **Ernie**
Bonnie and **Clyde**
Cheese and **crackers**
Cops and **robbers**
Dagwood and **Blondie**
Earth, Wind and **Fire**
Fibber McGee and **Molly**
Fred and **Wilma**
George and **Gracie**
Harpo, Groucho, Zeppo, and **Chico**
Hot and **cold**
In and **out**
Jack and **Jill**
Kiss and **Tell**

Liver and **onions**
Lone Ranger and **Tonto**
Macaroni and **cheese**
Peanut butter and **jelly**
Peter and the **Wolf**
Peter, Paul, and **Mary**
Porgy and **Bess**
Pots and **pans**
Reading, writing, and **'rithmatic**
Red, white and **blue**
Salt and **pepper**
Sears and **Roebuck**
Sodom and **Gomorrah**
Spencer Tracy and **Katherine Hepburn**
The birds and the **bees**
The Good, the Bad, and the **Ugly**
Up, up and **away**
War and **peace**
Washer and **dryer**

The "And" Game - Challenge Edition

Assault and _____

Atcheson, _____, and the _____ __

Baltimore and _____

Bell, Book, and _____

Birds and _____

Bogie and _____

Borrowed and _____

Bread and _____

Burns and _____

Cat and _____

Comedy and _____

Cream and _____

Fast and _____

Field and _____

Footloose and _____ _____

Frankie and _____

Fric and _____

Gilbert and _____

Hook and _____

Hook, line and _____

Horse and _____

Ketchup and _____

Larry, Curly, and _____

Love and _____

Martin and _____

Mutt and _____

Oil and _____

Parsley, ____, _____ and _____

Pat and _____

Positive and _____

Raining cats and _____

Rock and _____

Rogers and _____

Rough and _____

Samson and _____

Savings and _____

Slow and _____

Snap, _____ and _____

Snow White and the _____

Stars and _____

Starsky and _____

The Pit and the _____

Tippecanoe and _____

Tooth and _____

Tortoise and the _____

Vanilla and _____

NOW IT'S YOUR TURN!

_____ and _____   _____ and _____

_____ and _____   _____ and _____

_____ and _____   _____ and _____

_____ and _____   _____ and _____

_____ and _____   _____ and _____

_____ and _____   _____ and _____

OPTIMAL WELL-BEING FOR SENIOR ADULTS I

The "And" Game - Challenge Edition
Leader's Guide

PURPOSE
To engage thinking skills with challenging brain-boosting activities.

POSSIBLE NAMES OF SESSIONS
- *Think Again!*
- *AND So On!*
- *Come On … You Can Do It!*

BACKGROUND INFORMATION
Cognitive activities can be success-oriented, stimulating, and fun. The prompts that come before the "and" are from a variety of sources including TV, books, songs, poems, food, childhood games, and idioms. This edition is for those who were very successful at the first *"AND" Game. (page 119).*

ACTIVITY
1. Introduce the concept of using the brain like a muscle. The brain needs exercising, and the way to do it is by challenging it.
2. Distribute handouts and pens. Instruct group members to write the best answers on the lines. Even though there are many answers that might be right, there is one preferred answer. Allow group members as much time as it takes to complete the handout. Use the key at the bottom of the page to check for answers.
3. Share responses.
4. Ask group to think of new *Now It's Your Turn* AND words – and to challenge each other.
5. Process the value of challenging the mind in fun and enjoyable ways.

VARIATIONS
1) Use as a timed activity, giving the winner a round of applause.
2) Play in pairs with one person giving the clues and the other one answering. Allow one hint if the guesser doesn't get it right on the first try.

ANSWER KEY

Assault and **battery**
Atcheson, **Topeka,** and the **Sante Fe**
Baltimore and **Ohio**
Bell, Book, and **Candle**
Birds and **bees**
Bogie and **Bacall**
Borrowed and **blue**
Bread and **butter**
Burns and **Allen**
Cat and **dog**
Comedy and **tragedy**
Cream and **sugar**
Fast and **furious**
Field and **stream**
Footloose and **fancy free**
Frankie and **Johnnie**
Fric and **Frac**
Gilbert and **Sullivan**
Hook and **ladder**
Hook, line and **sinker**
Horse and **carriage**
Ketchup and **mustard**
Larry, Curly, and **Moe**

Love and **marriage**
Martin and **Lewis**
Mutt and **Jeff**
Oil and **vinegar**
Parsley, **sage, rosemary, and thyme**
Pat and **Mike**
Positive and **negative**
Raining cats and **dogs**
Rock and **roll**
Rogers and **Hammerstein**
Rough and **ready**
Samson and **Delilah**
Savings and **loan**
Slow and **steady**
Snap, **crackle** and **pop**
Snow White and the **Seven Dwarfs**
Stars and **stripes**
Starsky and **Hutch**
The Pit and the **Pendulum**
Tippecanoe and **Tyler, Too**
Tooth and **Nail**
Tortoise and the **Hare**
Vanilla and **Chocolate**

Topic X — THINKING SKILLS

CURRENT EVENTS!

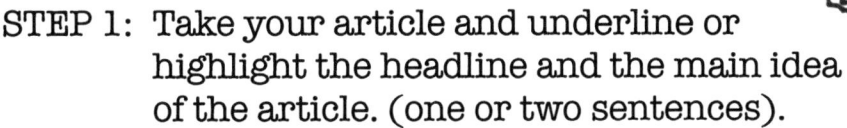

It is very important to know what's going on around you.

STEP 1: Take your article and underline or highlight the headline and the main idea of the article. (one or two sentences).

STEP 2: Circle your responses below, and fill in the lines.

1. Summarize the article in one or two sentences. _____
   _____
   _____
   _____

2. I **would / would not** recommend this article to someone else.

   If you said that you would recommend it, to whom would you recommend it?
   _____

   If you said that you would not recommend it, why wouldn't you recommend it?
   _____
   _____

3. I thought the article **was / was not** very well written.

4. I learned something from reading this. **Yes / No**

   If you said yes, what did you learn?
   _____

5. Do you have questions after reading the article? List them here.
   _____
   _____
   _____
   _____
   _____

6. What is your favorite part of the newspaper? _____
   _____
   _____

CURRENT EVENTS!
Leader's Guide

PURPOSE
To engage cognitively about what is happening in the world with possible benefits of reality orientation, drawing attention away from an internal focus and moving towards an external focus, and developing interesting conversation and social interaction on relevant topics.

POSSIBLE NAMES OF SESSIONS
- *What's Going On?*
- *Staying Current*
- *Being in the Know!*

BACKGROUND INFORMATION
There are many reasons people lose touch with the outside world, including disinterest, lack of stimulation, or self-focus to the exclusion of everything else. Newspapers are perfect, non-threatening therapeutic medias to use to re-enter the world! Talking about the news in a group setting can be a comfortable and shared experience. A structured, success-oriented session may pique an interest and provide a common ground for discussion.

ACTIVITY
1. Before session, read several articles in the local newspaper. Choose a wide variety of articles, making sure there are more than the number of people in the group, and that they are varied in interest and difficulty. Choose what you think might be of interest to your population and give choices of weather, movie reviews, sports, local politics, national news, and an international story.
   Articles should be short enough to keep the person's attention and long enough to report on.
2. Explain group purpose in a language that group members can understand and find meaningful.
3. Distribute handouts, highlighters, and pens.
4. Introduce articles by interest and abilities.
5. Allow group members to present the information written on the handout.
6. Ask each group member to present the information written on the handout.
7. Facilitate conversations among group members as curiosity or interests are piqued.

VARIATIONS
1) Distribute favorite cartoons from the newspaper as a fun ending for the group.
2) Talk about what might be good topics for conversation starters in the next few days based on the days' discussion.

NOTES
_____
_____
_____
_____
_____
_____
_____
_____
_____
_____

Topic X — THINKING SKILLS

Which / Witch is It?

Homophones = words that sound the same but are spelled differently.

Scoring: 1 point for each blank

Ant / _____
Ate / _____
Bare / _____
Be / _____
Beach / _____
Blue / _____
Bore / _____
Bow / _____
Byte / _____
Dear / _____
Die / _____
Flea / _____
Foul / _____
Grate / _____
Grown / _____
Hair / _____
Hear / _____
Hi / _____
Hole / _____
I / _____

Knight / _____
Know / _____
Lien / _____
Lo / _____
Loan / _____
Mite / _____
Pane / _____
Pi / _____
Red / _____
Sale / _____
Sea / _____
Sell / _____
Sew / _____
Soul / _____
Tee / _____
There / _____
Threw / _____
Toe / _____
Wear / _____
Witch / _____

TOTAL POINTS _____

Which / Witch is It?
Leader's Guide

PURPOSE
To stimulate thinking by using homophones as a brain-boosting prompt.

POSSIBLE NAMES OF SESSIONS
- *Same Sound – Different Meaning*
- *Sound-Alikes*
- *Boost Your Brain*

BACKGROUND INFORMATION
Challenging our brains in different ways is important for overall brain health and thinking skills. Using homophones is interesting and fun! We read and hear them all day, but many go unnoticed until we actually think about them.

ACTIVITY
1. Introduce topic by giving homophone examples: road and rode, peace and piece, knows and nose.
2. Distribute handouts and pens.
3. Give group fifteen to twenty minutes to complete.
4. Score to determine winner and give token prize or a rousing round of applause.
5. Celebrate everyone's thinking powers!
6. Discuss ways of actively engaging the brain and how to avoid being in a rut. (e.g., doing crossword puzzles, and something else for the brain, every day!).

VARIATIONS
1) Offer this as a timed exercise for added competitive spirit. First player with 40 points wins.
2) Use as a team game, everyone in the team gets a handout, but only one recorder writes answers for group. Give all groups a predetermined amount of time to complete the handout. Team with the most points wins!

ANSWER KEY

Ant / **Aunt**	Knight / **Night**
Ate / **Eight**	Know / **No**
Bare / **Bear**	Lien / **Lean**
Be / **Bee**	Lo / **Low**
Beach / **Beech**	Loan / **Lone**
Blue / **Blew**	Mite / **Might**
Bore / **Boar**	Pane / **Pain**
Bow / **Bough**	Pi / **Pie**
Byte / **Bite**	Red / **Read**
Dear / **Deer**	Sale / **Sail**
Die / **Dye**	Sea / **See**
Flea / **Flee**	Sell / **Cell**
Foul / **Fowl**	Sew / **So** / **Sow**
Grate / **Great**	Soul / **Sole**
Grown / **Groan**	Tee / **Tea**
Hair / **Hare**	There / **Their**
Hear / **Here**	Threw / **Through**
Hi / **High**	Toe / **Tow**
Hole / **Whole**	Wear / **Ware**
I / **Eye**	Witch / **Which**

Topic X — THINKING SKILLS

Mental Toughness – The Thinker Quiz

1. Does France have a fourth of July? _____

2. If a woman lives in Richmond, VA., why can't she be buried west of the Missouri River. _____

3. On average, how many birthdays does the average person have? _____

4. If you had only one match and needed to light a candle, a wood burning stove, a kerosene lamp, an oil burner, and a grill – which one would you light first? _____

5. Some words have five letters, some words have four letters. How many words have one letter? _____

6. If a doctor gave you six pain pills and told you to take one every half hour, how long would they last? _____

7. How far can a deer run into a cornfield? _____

8. If I hold two US coins which total thirty cents in value, and one is not a quarter, what are the two coins?

9. A woman had twelve cats; all but four ran away. How many did she have left? _____

10. Two girls were playing chess. They played seven games and each won the same number of games (there were no ties). How do you figure this? _____

11. Take three oranges from four oranges. What do you have? _____

12. Is it illegal for a man in China to marry his widow's sister? _____

OPTIMAL WELL-BEING FOR SENIOR ADULTS I

Mental Toughness – The Thinker Quiz
Leader's Guide

PURPOSE
To increase thought-processing and group involvement by answering questions, listening, and sharing.

POSSIBLE NAMES OF SESSIONS
- *It's So Hard to Focus Sometimes!*
- *Brain Exercises*
- *Thought-full Questions*

BACKGROUND INFORMATION
Answering challenging questions can be used as an entire activity or as a warm up activity to facilitate critical thinking and increase concentration to task. It also teaches the value of listening skills and attention to detail.

ACTIVITY
1. Distribute handouts and pens.
2. Give group ten minutes to individually complete the handouts.
3. Divide group into smaller groups of two to three members. Allow them time to discuss their answers and decide on the right one.
4. Ask smaller groups to each share their best answer for each question.
5. Use ANSWER KEY to clarify, if needed. Paper and pen might also be helpful in explaining challenging ones.
6. Give a small token reward for the team with most correct answers.
7. Ask group members for reasons this activity might be useful or helpful.
8. Engage in a discussion of how to continue to challenge our minds.

VARIATIONS
1) Ask group members if they have any brainteasers to add to the list. Collect group members' contributions for future groups!
2) Distribute handouts and only give group members five minutes to complete as many as they can.

ANSWER KEY
1. YES! All countries have a fourth of July … and a fifth, and a sixth, etc.
2. She is still alive.
3. ONE – the rest are just celebrations of the birth.
4. The match.
5. All of them!
6. Two and a half hours.
7. Halfway, he would then be running out.
8. One quarter and one nickel (it says that only one isn't a quarter).
9. Four
10. They weren't playing each other.
11. Three oranges.
12. If he were living, how would he have a widow?

NOTES
_____
_____
_____
_____
_____

Topic XI
BONUS
Table of Contents and Corresponding Goals for Each Section

"Aging is not lost youth but a new stage of opportunity and strength.."
~ Betty Friedan

CERTIFICATE 131
To acknowledge an individual's accomplishment.

Mandala 133
To explore relaxation through coloring.

OPTIMAL WELL-BEING FOR SENIOR ADULTS I

CERTIFICATE
Leader's Guide

PURPOSE
To acknowledge an individual's accomplishment.

POSSIBLE NAMES OF SESSIONS
- *Graduation Day*
- *A Proper Send Off!*
- *Gifts for You*

BACKGROUND INFORMATION
Everyone wants and needs to be recognized, even if they won't admit it! This certificate gives a tangible and memorable gift to those who have shown the dedication, perseverance, and commitment to complete a program.

ACTIVITY
1. Photocopy this certificate (preferably using a light colored paper) to recognize and acknowledge the group members who have completed the program.
2. Ask staff to sign notes in the blank spaces to wish them well.
3. Present the certificates, giving specific praise for a job well done.

VARIATIONS
Before awarding the certificates, ask each group member to give a "gift" to the graduates. It can be anything at all as long as it does not cost money and is heartfelt. *(Example: tranquility, travel to your heart's delight, be pain-free, sobriety, etc.)*

NOTES
_____
_____
_____
_____
_____
_____
_____
_____
_____
_____
_____
_____
_____
_____
_____
_____
_____
_____

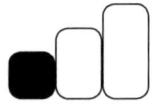

Mandala
Leader's Guide

PURPOSE

To explore the relaxation of coloring a mandala.

POSSIBLE NAMES OF SESSIONS
- *Relaxation*
- *Creative Expression*
- *Mandala Mindfulness*

BACKGROUND INFORMATION

Coloring can be relaxing, meditative, and enhance mindfulness by focusing on just the act of coloring. Learning how to gently redirect the mind to a single activity is a worthwhile and lifelong skill.

ACTIVITY

1. Photocopy this mandala and distribute it with gel pens, colored pencils, and crayons, for individual and group relaxation.
2. Try playing soft music.
3. Explain to participants that coloring can be meditative in nature.
4. Suggest that completed mandalas can be a gift to self or to others, as well as a wall hanging.

VARIATIONS

Use completed mandalas for the front of a group member's notebook or folder, on their door or bulletin board, or laminate two together as a placemat.

NOTES

_____
_____
_____
_____
_____
_____
_____
_____
_____
_____
_____
_____
_____
_____
_____
_____
_____
_____
_____
_____

Whole Person Associates is the leading publisher of training resources for professionals who empower people to create and maintain healthy lifestyles. Our creative resources will help you work effectively with your clients in the areas of stress management, wellness promotion, mental health, and life skills.

Please visit us at our web site: **WholePerson.com**. You can check out our entire line of products, place an order, request our print catalog, and sign up for our monthly special notifications.

Whole Person Associates
800-247-6789
Books@WholePerson.com